SNOOPY

(features as)

The Master Chef

Charles M. Schulz

PEANUTS is a registered trademark of United Feature Syndicate, Inc.
Based on the PEANUTS® comic strip by Charles M. Schulz.

Originally published in 1988 as 'Snoopy Stars as the Dog-Dish Gourmet'.
This edition published in the Year 2001 by Ravette Publishing.

Printed and bound in Great Britain
for Ravette Publishing Limited,
Unit 3, Tristar Centre,
Star Road, Partridge Green,
West Sussex RH13 8RA
by Cox & Wyman, Berkshire

ISBN: 1 84161 107 7

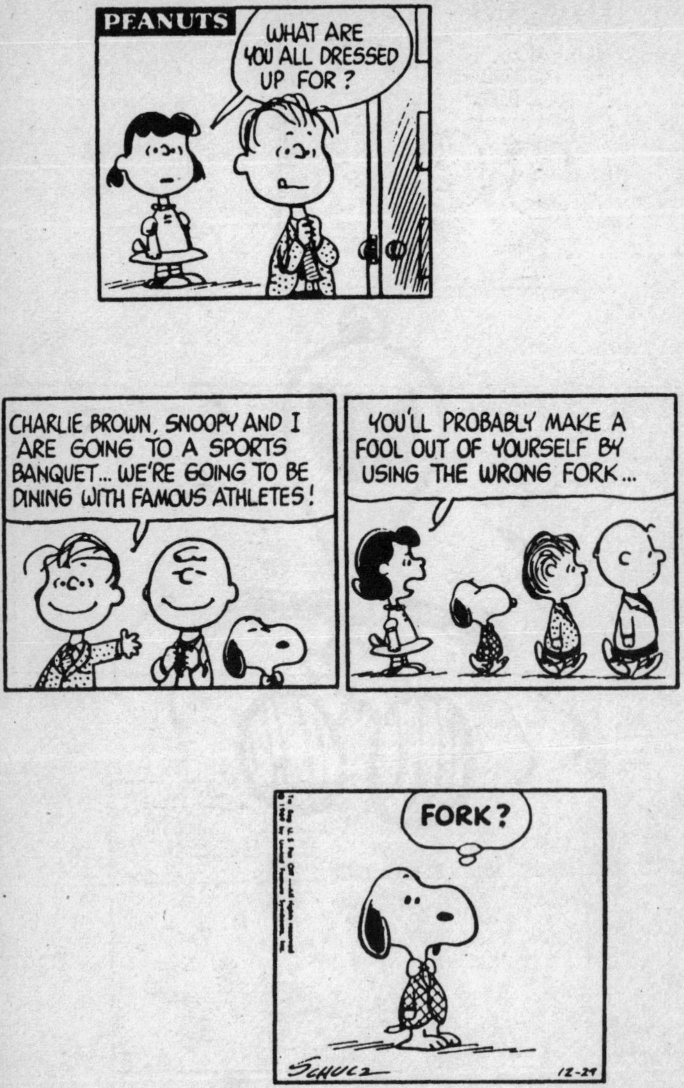
PEANUTS
WHAT ARE YOU ALL DRESSED UP FOR?
CHARLIE BROWN, SNOOPY AND I ARE GOING TO A SPORTS BANQUET... WE'RE GOING TO BE DINING WITH FAMOUS ATHLETES!
YOU'LL PROBABLY MAKE A FOOL OUT OF YOURSELF BY USING THE WRONG FORK...
FORK?
12-29

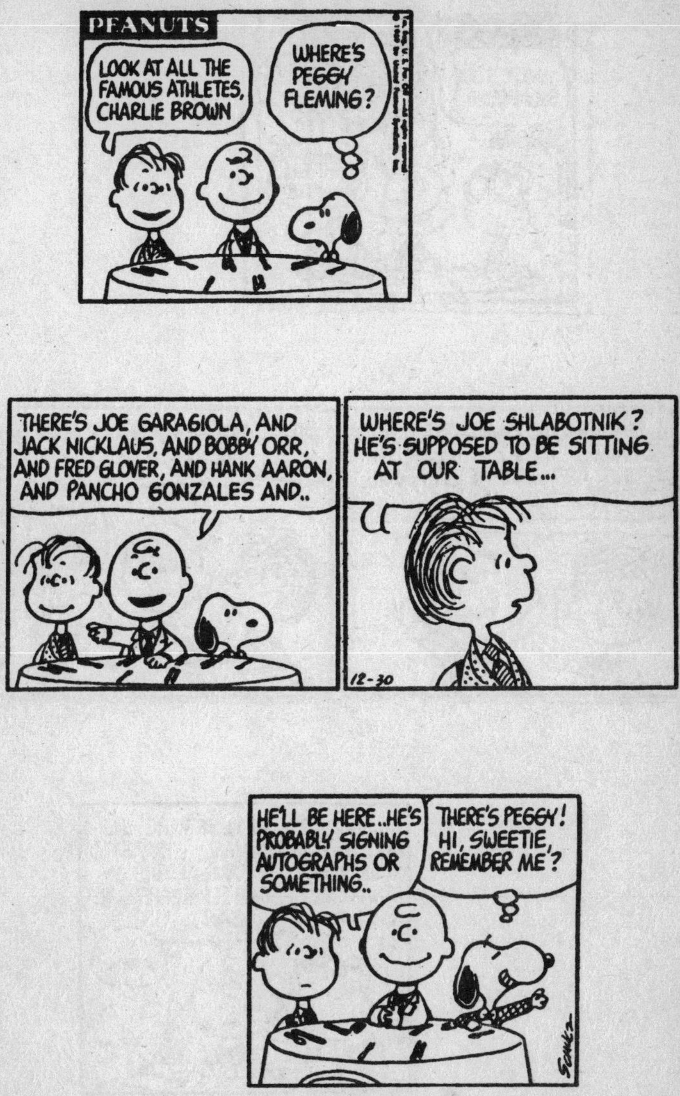
PEANUTS
LOOK AT ALL THE FAMOUS ATHLETES, CHARLIE BROWN
WHERE'S PEGGY FLEMING?
THERE'S JOE GARAGIOLA, AND JACK NICKLAUS, AND BOBBY ORR, AND FRED GLOVER, AND HANK AARON, AND PANCHO GONZALES AND..
WHERE'S JOE SHLABOTNIK? HE'S SUPPOSED TO BE SITTING AT OUR TABLE...
12-30
HE'LL BE HERE..HE'S PROBABLY SIGNING AUTOGRAPHS OR SOMETHING..
THERE'S PEGGY! HI, SWEETIE, REMEMBER ME?
SCHULZ

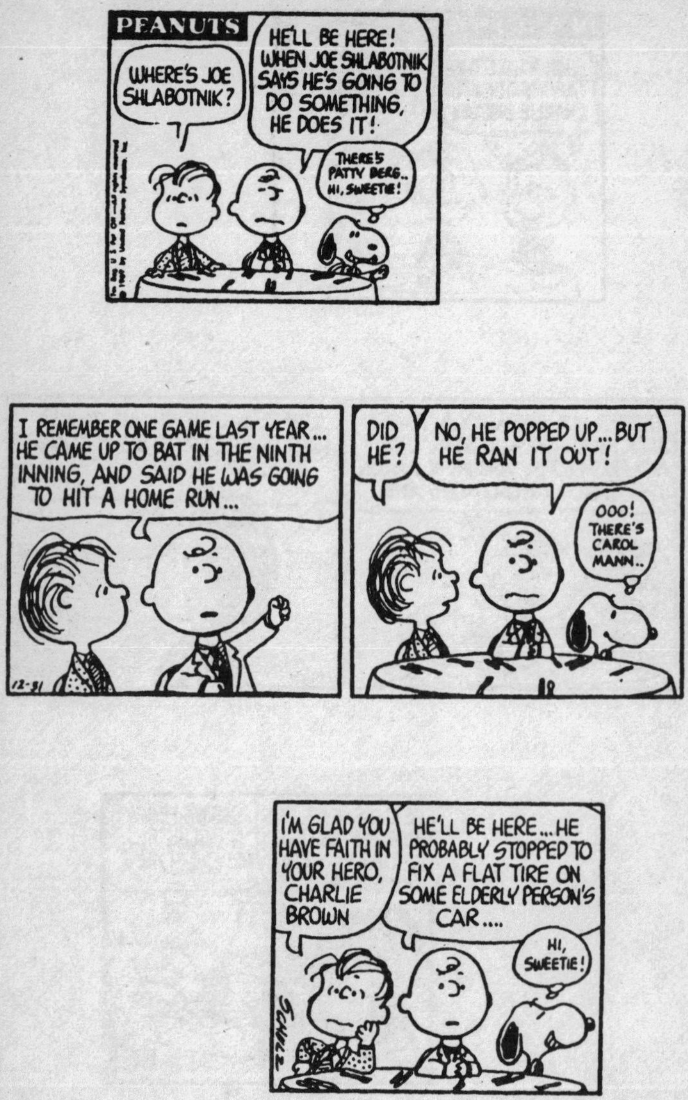
PEANUTS
WHERE'S JOE SHLABOTNIK?
HE'LL BE HERE! WHEN JOE SHLABOTNIK SAYS HE'S GOING TO DO SOMETHING, HE DOES IT!
THERE'S PATTY BERG.. HI, SWEETIE!
I REMEMBER ONE GAME LAST YEAR... HE CAME UP TO BAT IN THE NINTH INNING, AND SAID HE WAS GOING TO HIT A HOME RUN...
12-31
DID HE?
NO, HE POPPED UP... BUT HE RAN IT OUT!
OOO! THERE'S CAROL MANN..
I'M GLAD YOU HAVE FAITH IN YOUR HERO, CHARLIE BROWN
HE'LL BE HERE... HE PROBABLY STOPPED TO FIX A FLAT TIRE ON SOME ELDERLY PERSON'S CAR....
HI, SWEETIE!
SCHULZ

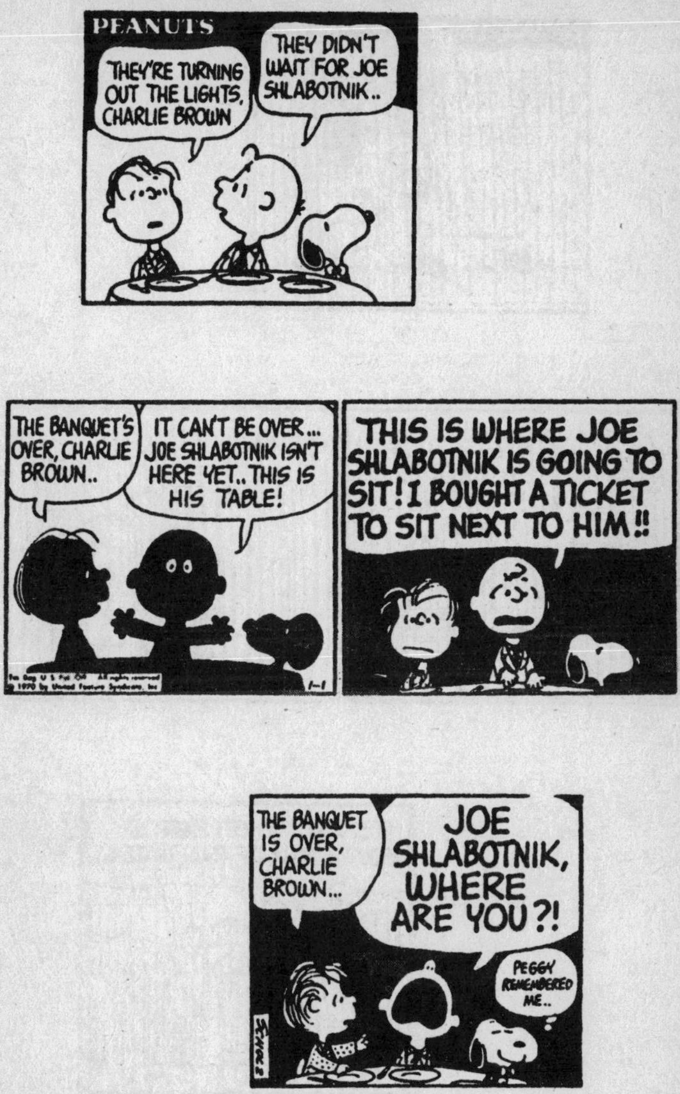
PEANUTS
THEY'RE TURNING OUT THE LIGHTS, CHARLIE BROWN
THEY DIDN'T WAIT FOR JOE SHLABOTNIK..
THE BANQUET'S OVER, CHARLIE BROWN..
IT CAN'T BE OVER... JOE SHLABOTNIK ISN'T HERE YET.. THIS IS HIS TABLE!
THIS IS WHERE JOE SHLABOTNIK IS GOING TO SIT! I BOUGHT A TICKET TO SIT NEXT TO HIM!!
THE BANQUET IS OVER, CHARLIE BROWN...
JOE SHLABOTNIK, WHERE ARE YOU?!
PEGGY REMEMBERED ME..

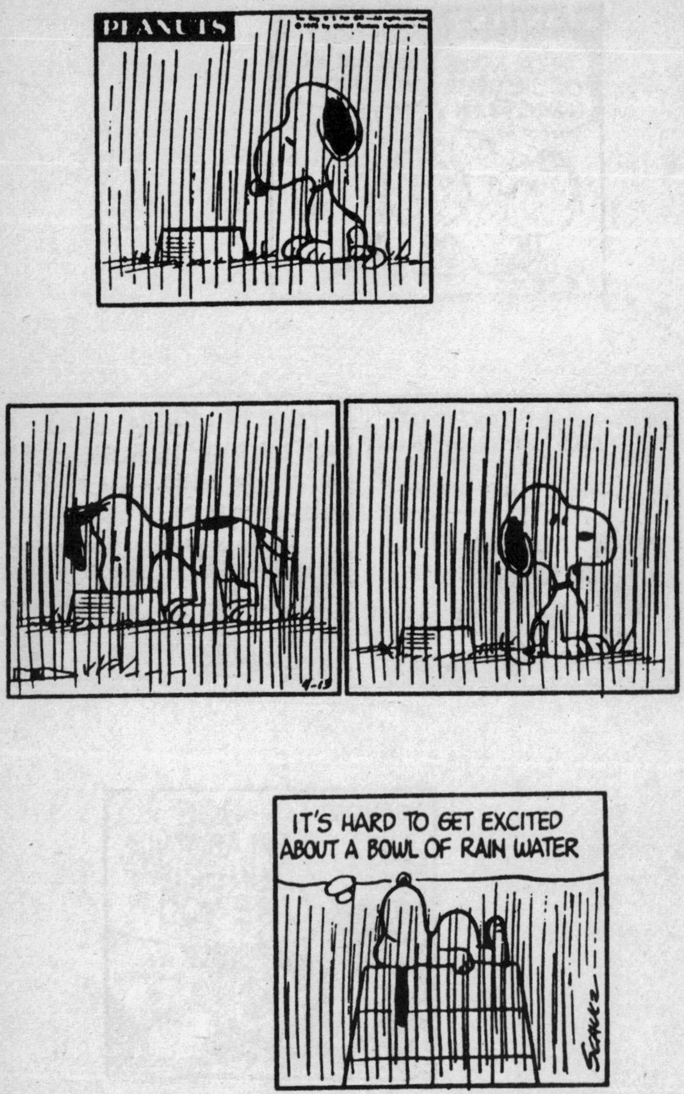
PEANUTS
IT'S HARD TO GET EXCITED ABOUT A BOWL OF RAIN WATER
SCHULZ

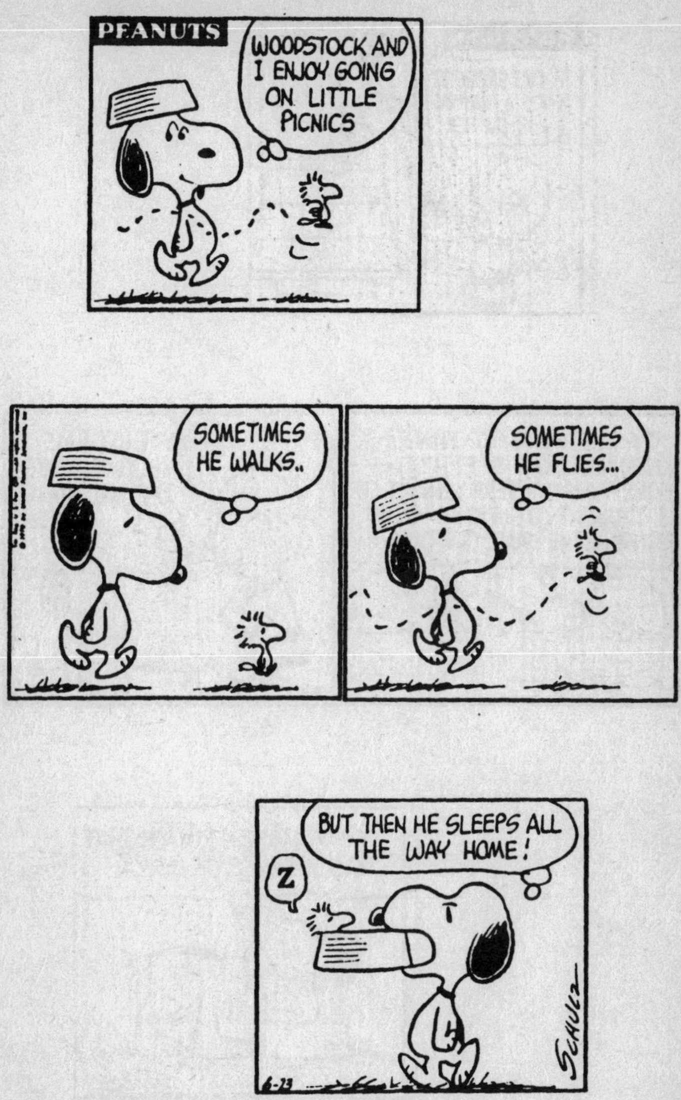
PEANUTS
WOODSTOCK AND I ENJOY GOING ON LITTLE PICNICS
SOMETIMES HE WALKS..
SOMETIMES HE FLIES...
Z
BUT THEN HE SLEEPS ALL THE WAY HOME!
SCHULZ

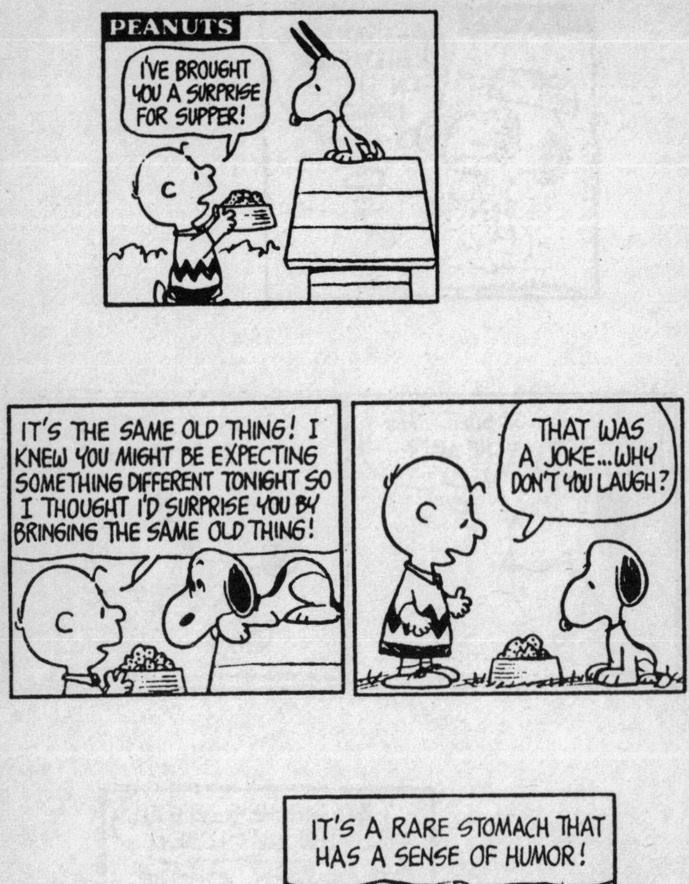
PEANUTS
I'VE BROUGHT YOU A SURPRISE FOR SUPPER!
IT'S THE SAME OLD THING! I KNEW YOU MIGHT BE EXPECTING SOMETHING DIFFERENT TONIGHT SO I THOUGHT I'D SURPRISE YOU BY BRINGING THE SAME OLD THING!
THAT WAS A JOKE...WHY DON'T YOU LAUGH?
IT'S A RARE STOMACH THAT HAS A SENSE OF HUMOR!
6-26
SCHULZ

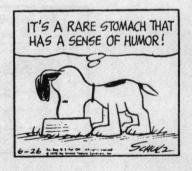

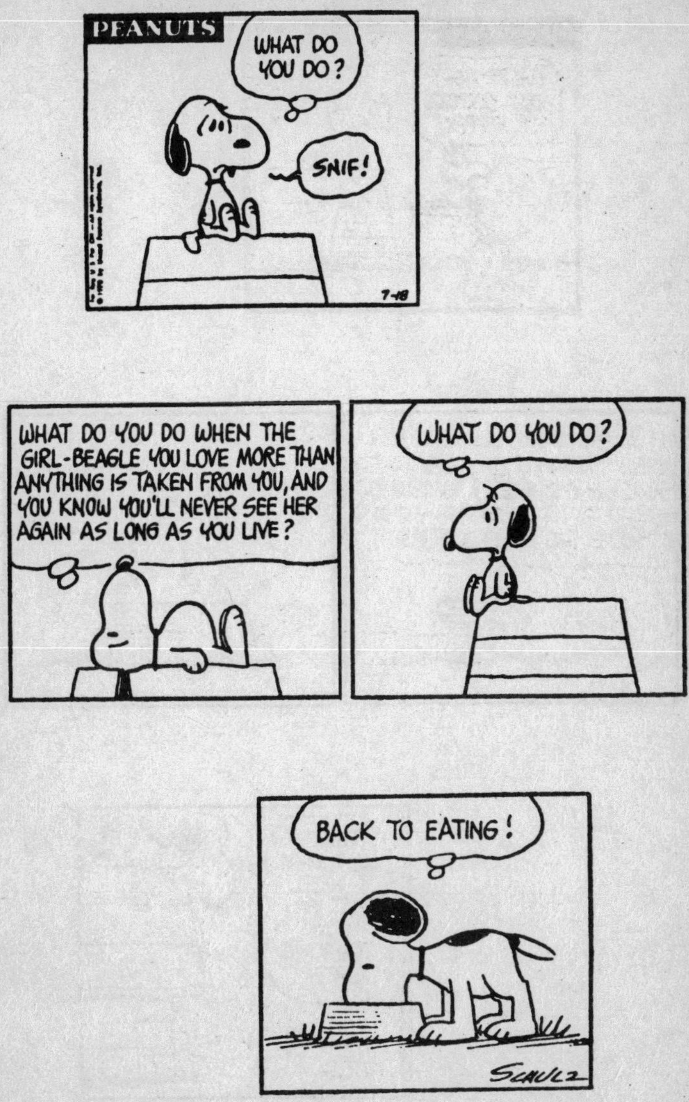
PEANUTS
WHAT DO YOU DO?
SNIF!
7-18
WHAT DO YOU DO WHEN THE GIRL-BEAGLE YOU LOVE MORE THAN ANYTHING IS TAKEN FROM YOU, AND YOU KNOW YOU'LL NEVER SEE HER AGAIN AS LONG AS YOU LIVE?
WHAT DO YOU DO?
BACK TO EATING!
SCHULZ

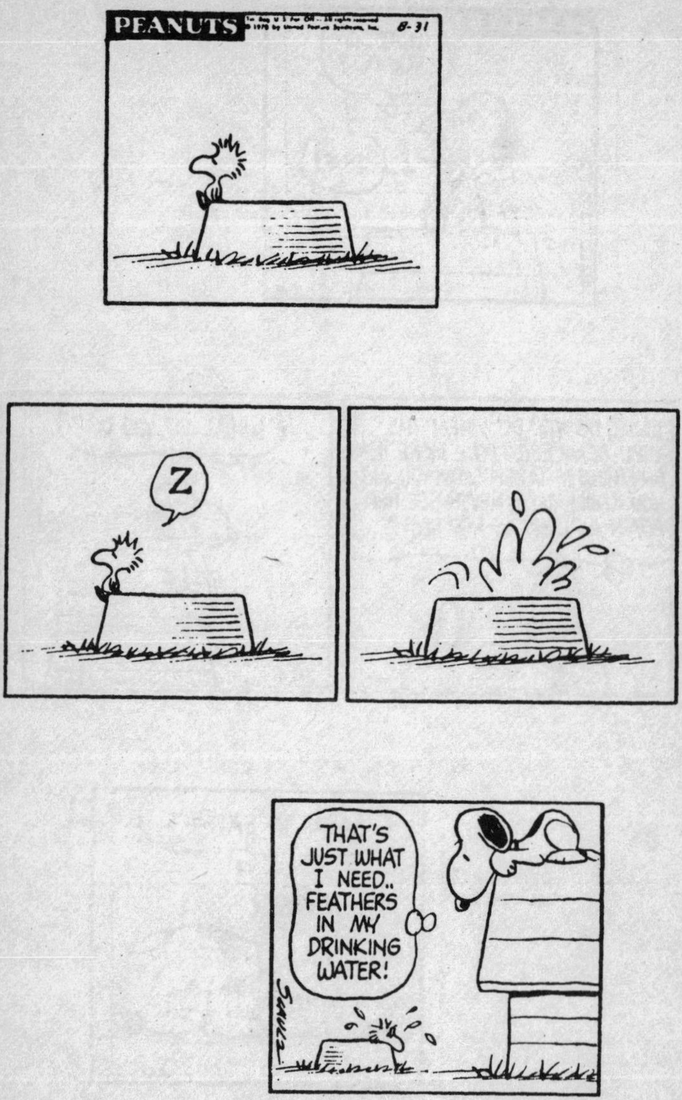
PEANUTS
8-31
Z
THAT'S JUST WHAT I NEED.. FEATHERS IN MY DRINKING WATER!
SCHULZ

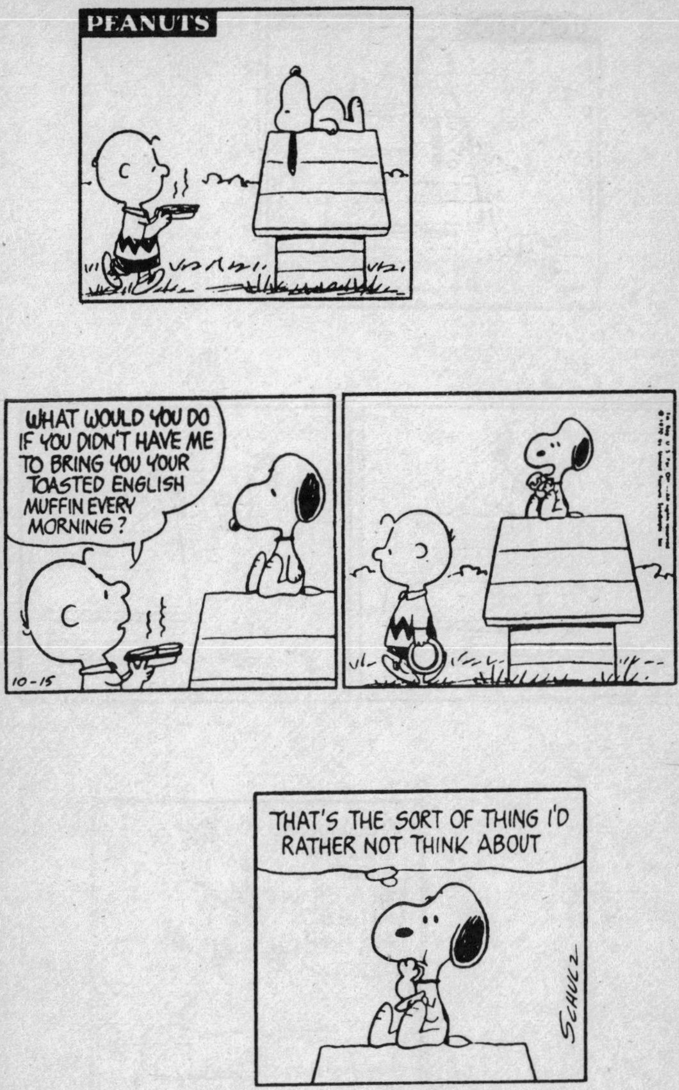
PEANUTS
WHAT WOULD YOU DO IF YOU DIDN'T HAVE ME TO BRING YOU YOUR TOASTED ENGLISH MUFFIN EVERY MORNING?
10-15
THAT'S THE SORT OF THING I'D RATHER NOT THINK ABOUT
SCHULZ

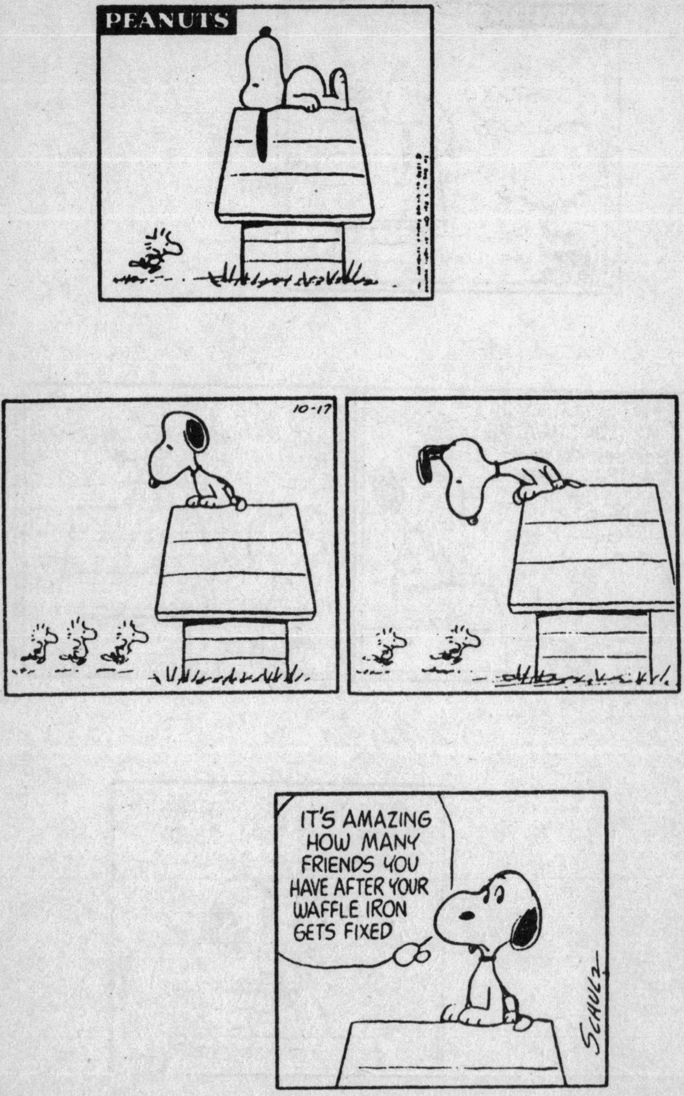
PEANUTS
10-17
IT'S AMAZING HOW MANY FRIENDS YOU HAVE AFTER YOUR WAFFLE IRON GETS FIXED
SCHULZ

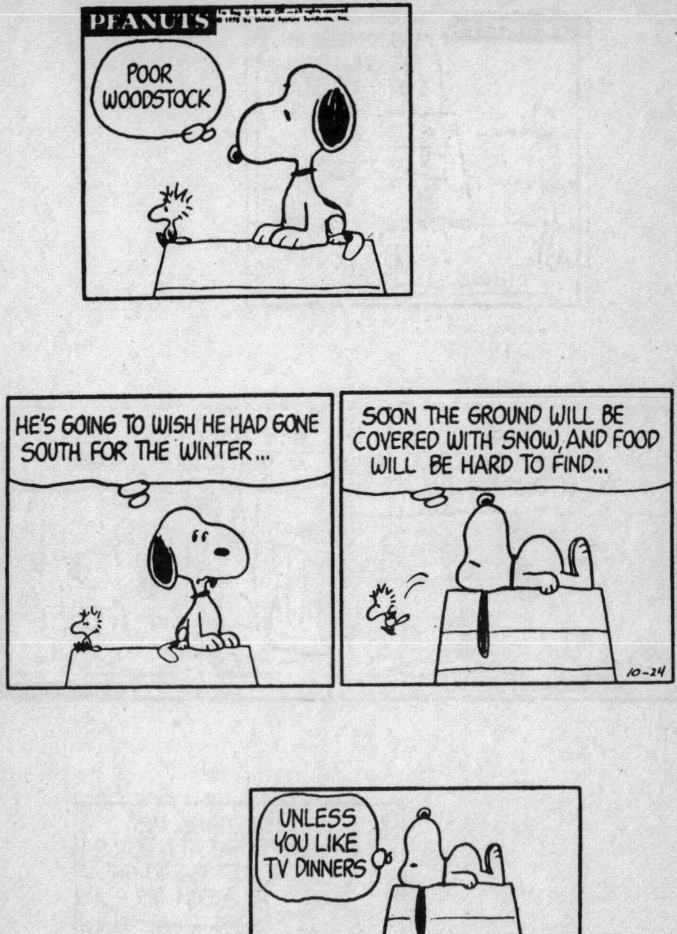
PEANUTS
POOR WOODSTOCK
HE'S GOING TO WISH HE HAD GONE SOUTH FOR THE WINTER...
SOON THE GROUND WILL BE COVERED WITH SNOW, AND FOOD WILL BE HARD TO FIND...
10-24
UNLESS YOU LIKE TV DINNERS
SCHULZ

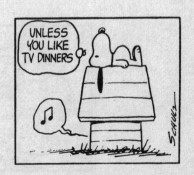

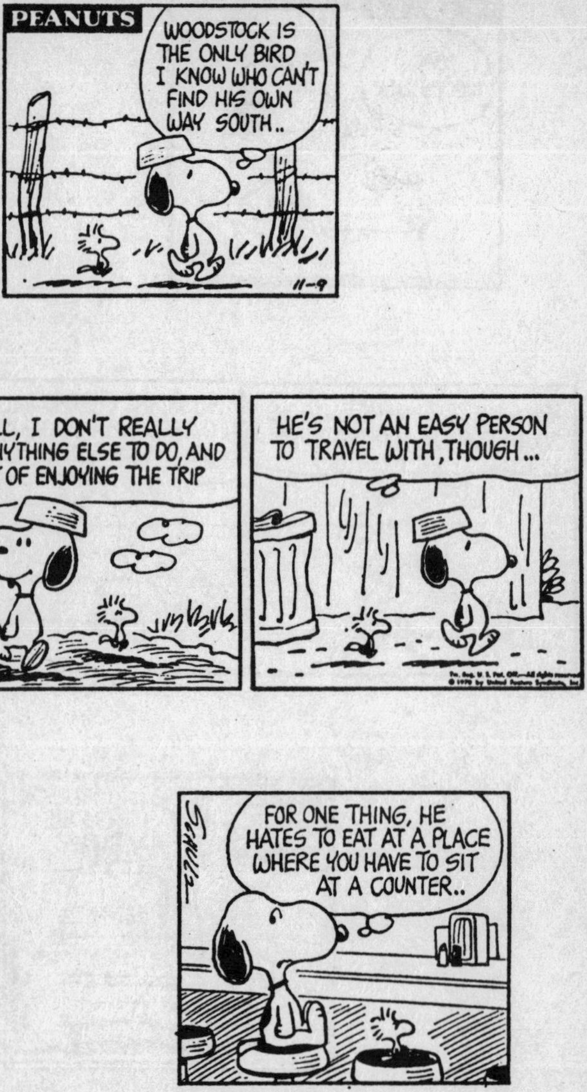
PEANUTS
WOODSTOCK IS THE ONLY BIRD I KNOW WHO CAN'T FIND HIS OWN WAY SOUTH..
11-9
OH, WELL, I DON'T REALLY HAVE ANYTHING ELSE TO DO, AND I'M SORT OF ENJOYING THE TRIP
HE'S NOT AN EASY PERSON TO TRAVEL WITH, THOUGH...
SCHULZ
FOR ONE THING, HE HATES TO EAT AT A PLACE WHERE YOU HAVE TO SIT AT A COUNTER..

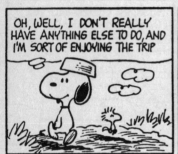

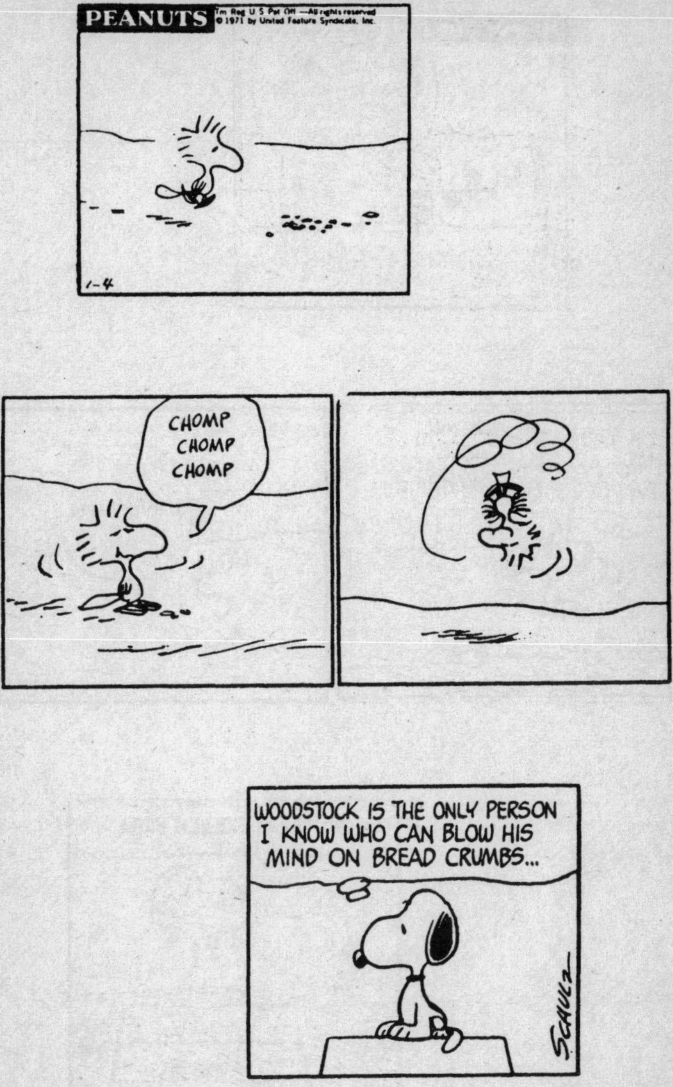
PEANUTS
Tm Reg U.S. Pat Off —All rights reserved © 1971 by United Feature Syndicate, Inc.
1-4
CHOMP CHOMP CHOMP
WOODSTOCK IS THE ONLY PERSON I KNOW WHO CAN BLOW HIS MIND ON BREAD CRUMBS...
SCHULZ

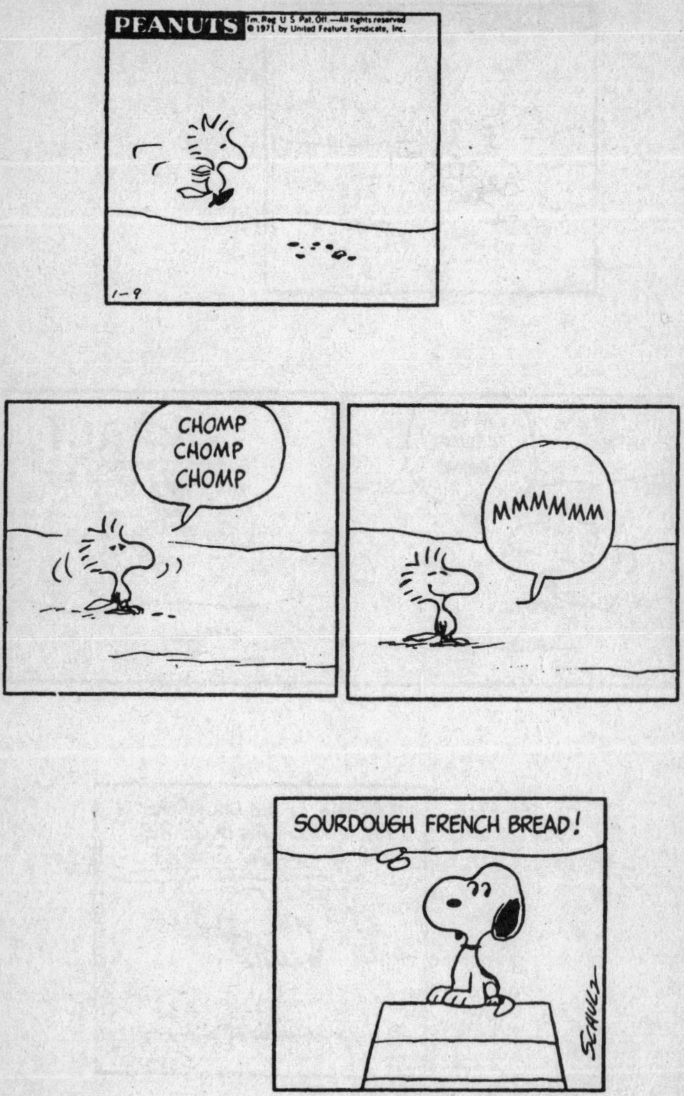
PEANUTS
Tm. Reg U S Pat. Off.—All rights reserved © 1971 by United Feature Syndicate, Inc.
1-9
CHOMP CHOMP CHOMP
MMMMMM
SOURDOUGH FRENCH BREAD!
SCHULZ

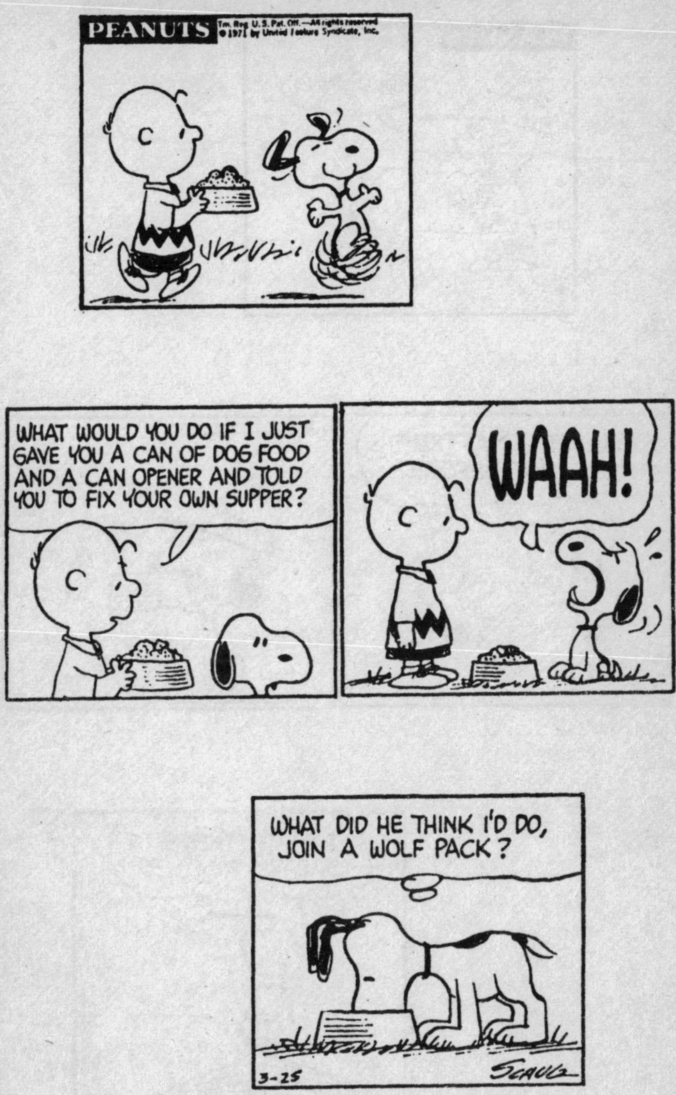
PEANUTS
Tm. Reg. U.S. Pat. Off.—All rights reserved © 1971 by United Feature Syndicate, Inc.
WHAT WOULD YOU DO IF I JUST GAVE YOU A CAN OF DOG FOOD AND A CAN OPENER AND TOLD YOU TO FIX YOUR OWN SUPPER?
WAAH!
WHAT DID HE THINK I'D DO, JOIN A WOLF PACK?
3-25
SCHULZ

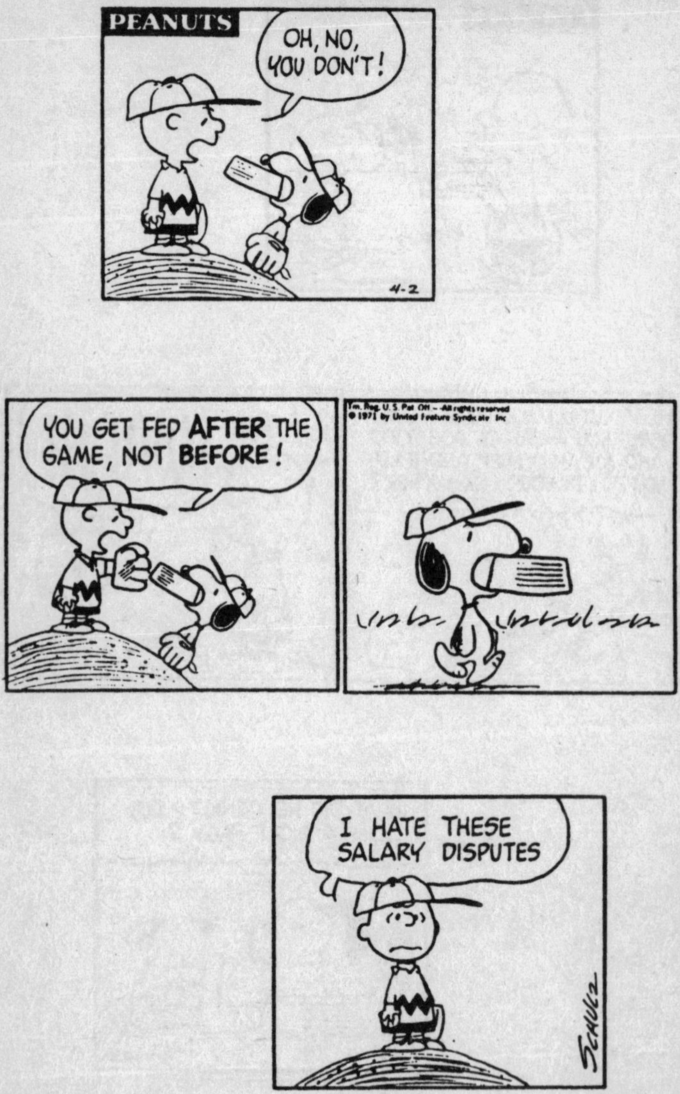
PEANUTS
OH, NO, YOU DON'T!
4-2
YOU GET FED AFTER THE GAME, NOT BEFORE!
Tm. Reg. U.S. Pat. Off.—All rights reserved
© 1971 by United Feature Syndicate, Inc.
I HATE THESE SALARY DISPUTES
SCHULZ

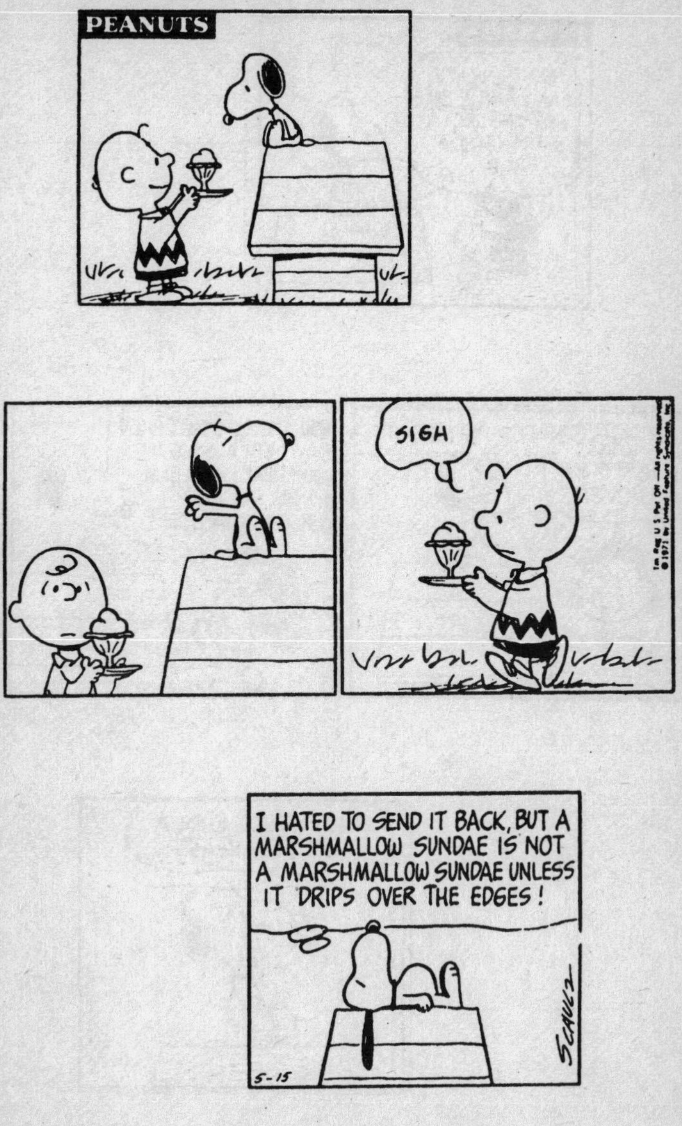
PEANUTS
SIGH
I HATED TO SEND IT BACK, BUT A MARSHMALLOW SUNDAE IS NOT A MARSHMALLOW SUNDAE UNLESS IT DRIPS OVER THE EDGES!
5-15
SCHULZ

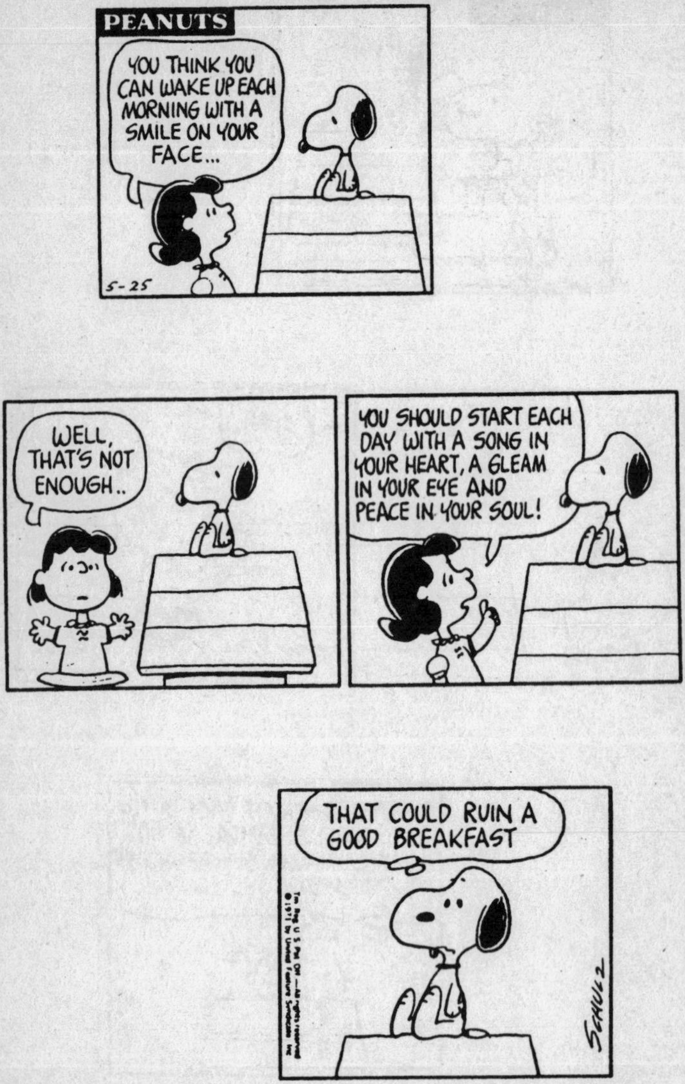
PEANUTS
YOU THINK YOU CAN WAKE UP EACH MORNING WITH A SMILE ON YOUR FACE...
5-25
WELL, THAT'S NOT ENOUGH..
YOU SHOULD START EACH DAY WITH A SONG IN YOUR HEART, A GLEAM IN YOUR EYE AND PEACE IN YOUR SOUL!
THAT COULD RUIN A GOOD BREAKFAST
Tm Reg U S Pat Off —All rights reserved
© 1971 by United Feature Syndicate Inc
SCHULZ

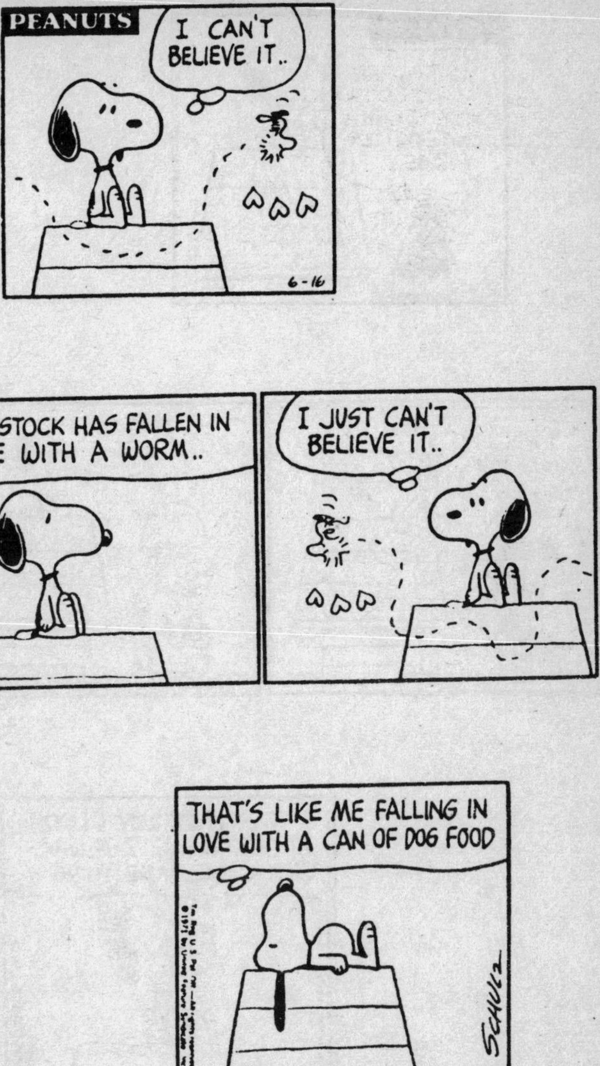
PEANUTS
I CAN'T BELIEVE IT..
6-16
WOODSTOCK HAS FALLEN IN LOVE WITH A WORM..
I JUST CAN'T BELIEVE IT..
THAT'S LIKE ME FALLING IN LOVE WITH A CAN OF DOG FOOD
SCHULZ

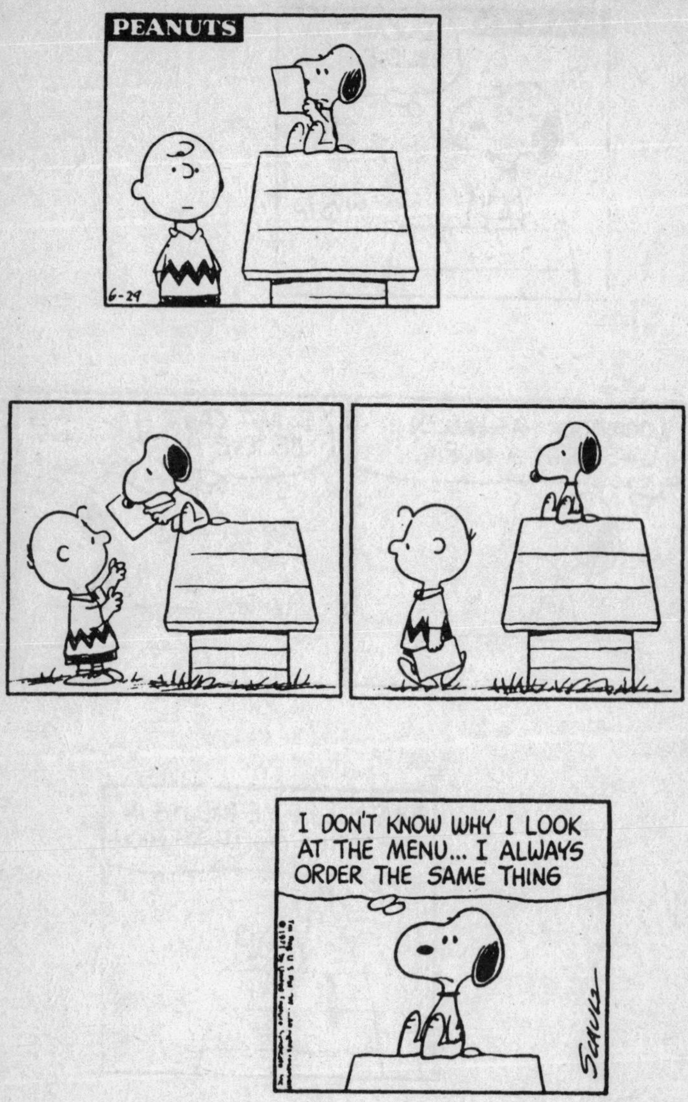
PEANUTS
6-29
I DON'T KNOW WHY I LOOK AT THE MENU... I ALWAYS ORDER THE SAME THING
SCHULZ

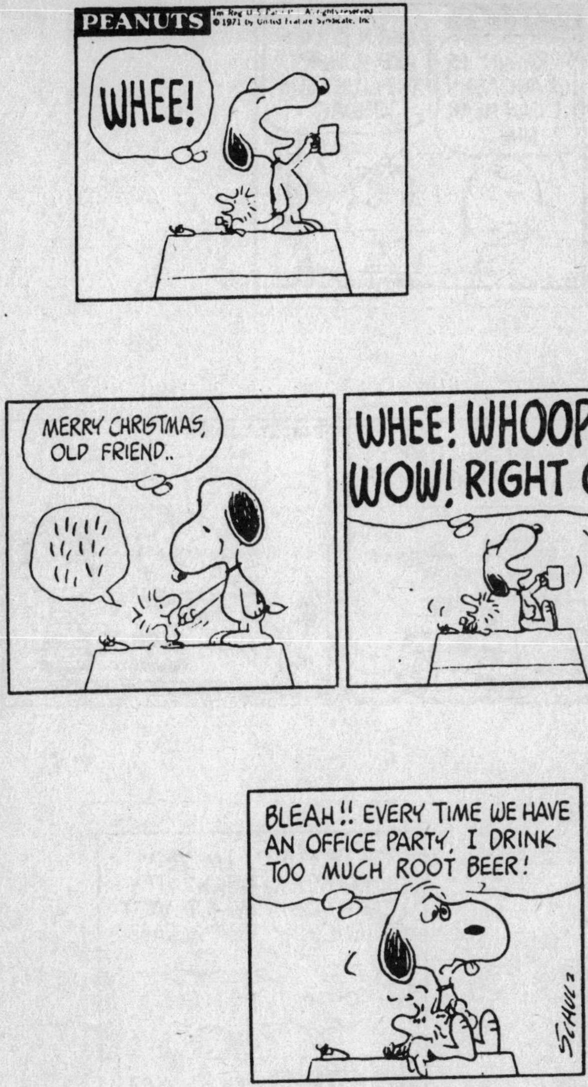
PEANUTS
WHEE!
MERRY CHRISTMAS, OLD FRIEND..
WHEE! WHOOPEE!! WOW! RIGHT ON!
12-24
BLEAH!! EVERY TIME WE HAVE AN OFFICE PARTY, I DRINK TOO MUCH ROOT BEER!
SCHULZ

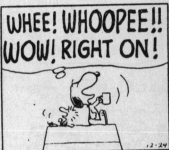

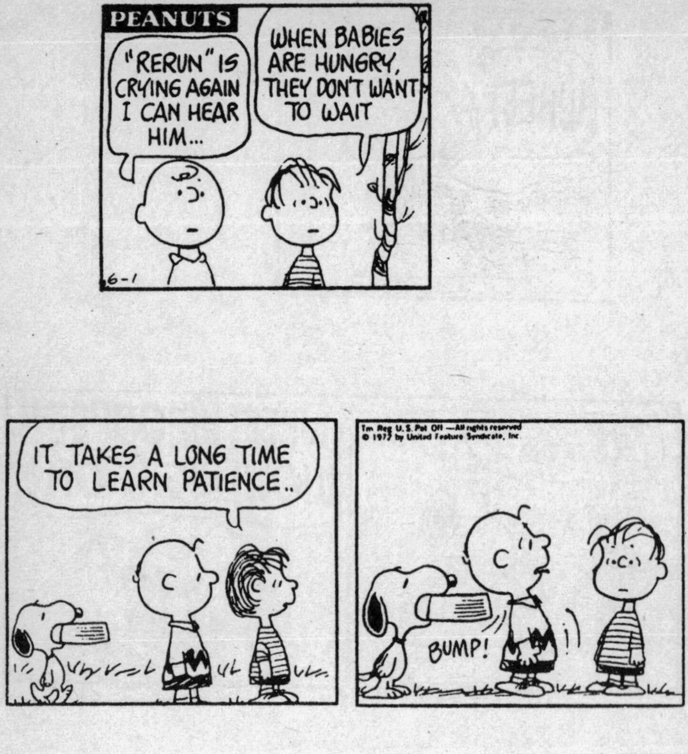
PEANUTS
"RERUN" IS CRYING AGAIN I CAN HEAR HIM...
WHEN BABIES ARE HUNGRY, THEY DON'T WANT TO WAIT
6-1
IT TAKES A LONG TIME TO LEARN PATIENCE..
Tm Reg U.S. Pat Off —All rights reserved © 1977 by United Feature Syndicate, Inc
BUMP!
SOME PEOPLE I KNOW NEVER LEARN ANY PATIENCE!
I'M VERY PATIENT...IT'S MY STOMACH THAT'S CRABBY!
SCHULZ

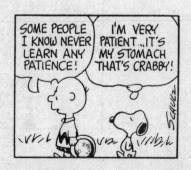

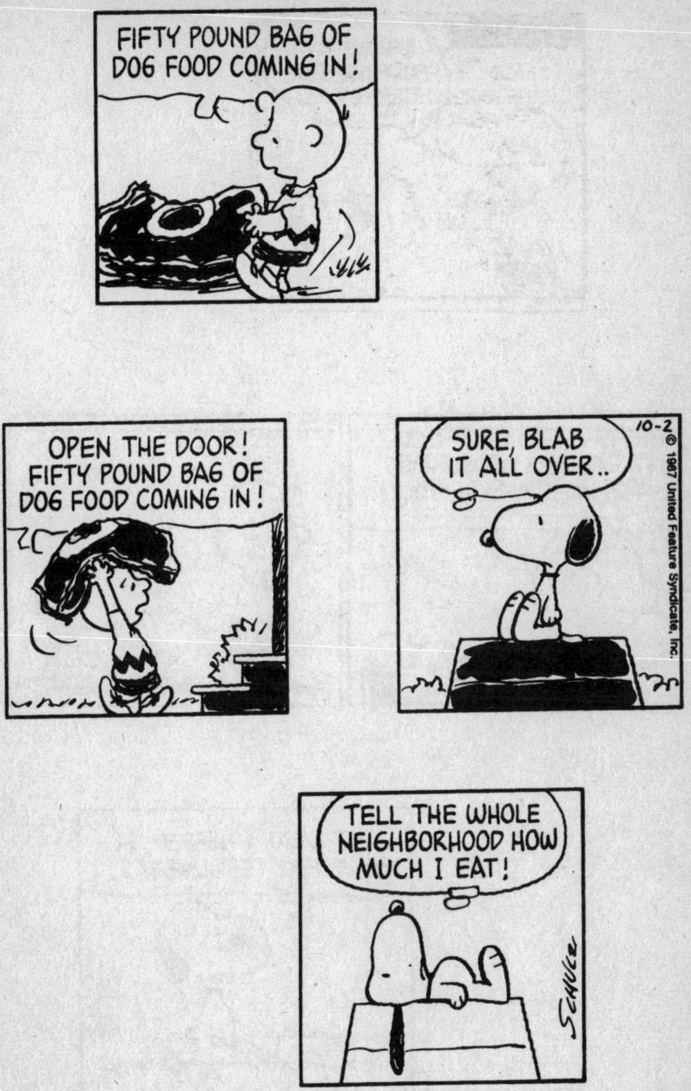
FIFTY POUND BAG OF DOG FOOD COMING IN!
OPEN THE DOOR! FIFTY POUND BAG OF DOG FOOD COMING IN!
SURE, BLAB IT ALL OVER..
10-2
© 1987 United Feature Syndicate, Inc.
TELL THE WHOLE NEIGHBORHOOD HOW MUCH I EAT!
SCHULZ

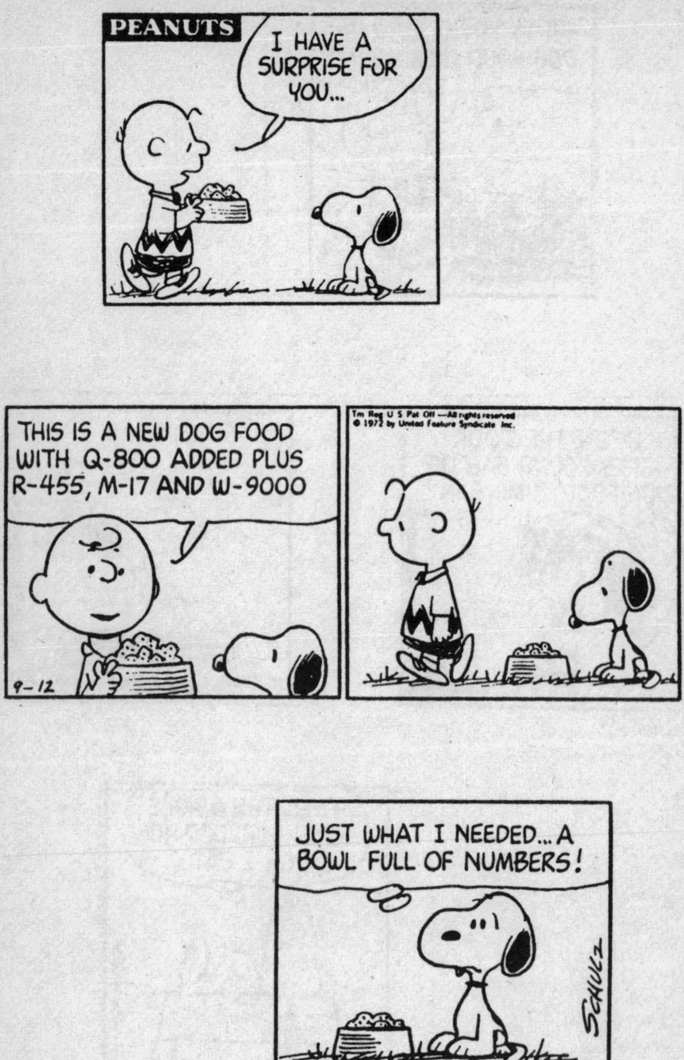
PEANUTS
I HAVE A SURPRISE FOR YOU...
THIS IS A NEW DOG FOOD WITH Q-800 ADDED PLUS R-455, M-17 AND W-9000
9-12
Tm Reg U S Pat Off —All rights reserved © 1972 by United Feature Syndicate Inc.
JUST WHAT I NEEDED... A BOWL FULL OF NUMBERS!
SCHULZ

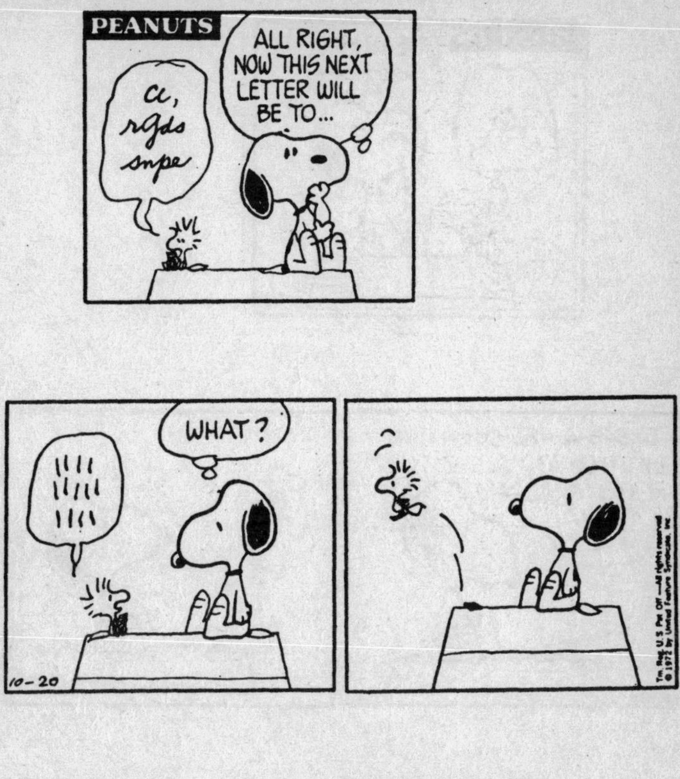
PEANUTS
ci, rgds snpe
ALL RIGHT, NOW THIS NEXT LETTER WILL BE TO...
WHAT?
SEED BREAK!
10-20
Tm. Reg. U.S. Pat. Off.—All rights reserved © 1972 by United Feature Syndicate, Inc
SCHULZ

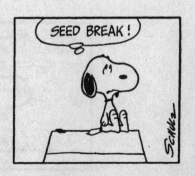

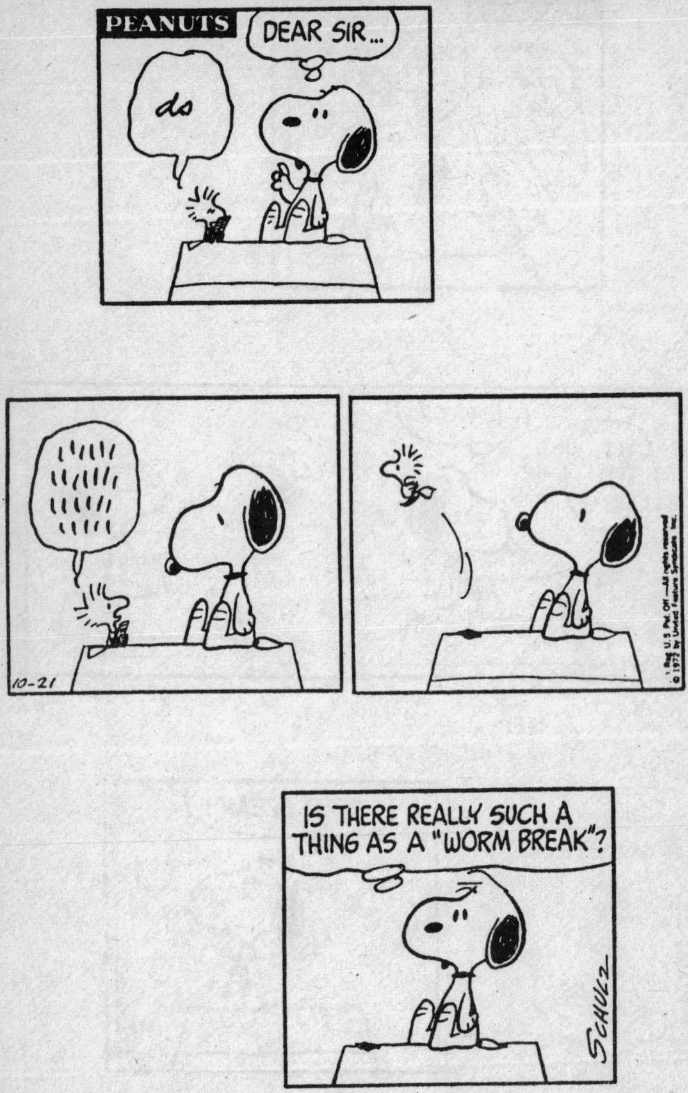
PEANUTS
DEAR SIR...
10-21
Reg. U.S. Pat. Off.—All rights reserved © 1972 by United Feature Syndicate, Inc.
IS THERE REALLY SUCH A THING AS A "WORM BREAK"?
SCHULZ

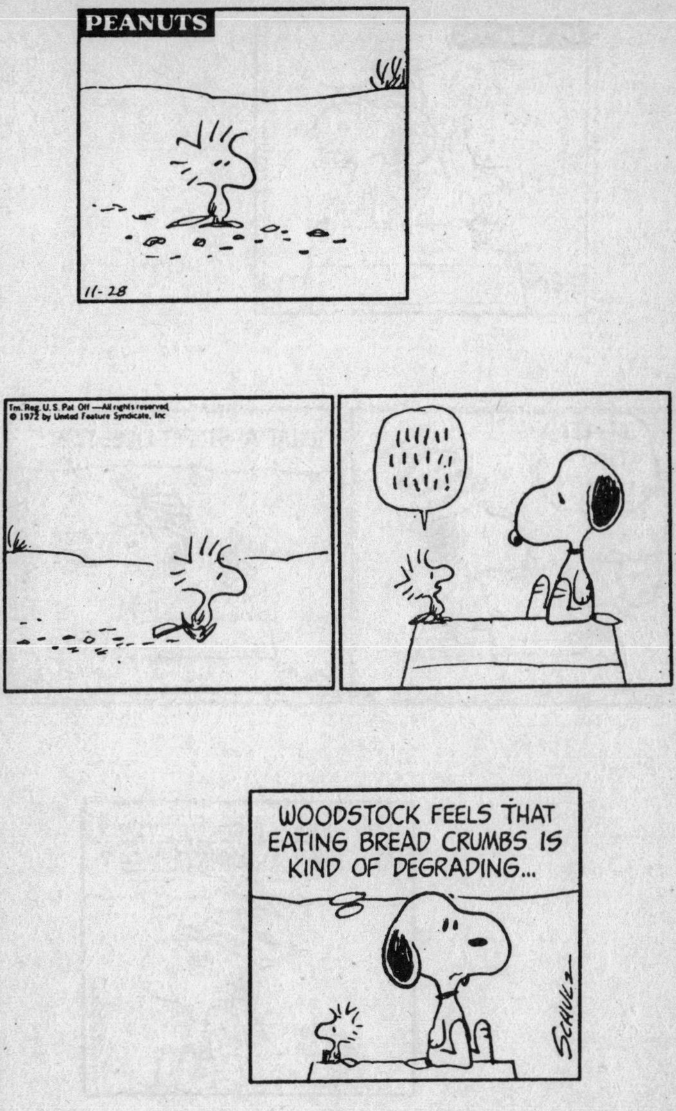
PEANUTS
11-28
Tm. Reg. U.S. Pat. Off.—All rights reserved
© 1972 by United Feature Syndicate, Inc
WOODSTOCK FEELS THAT EATING BREAD CRUMBS IS KIND OF DEGRADING...
SCHULZ

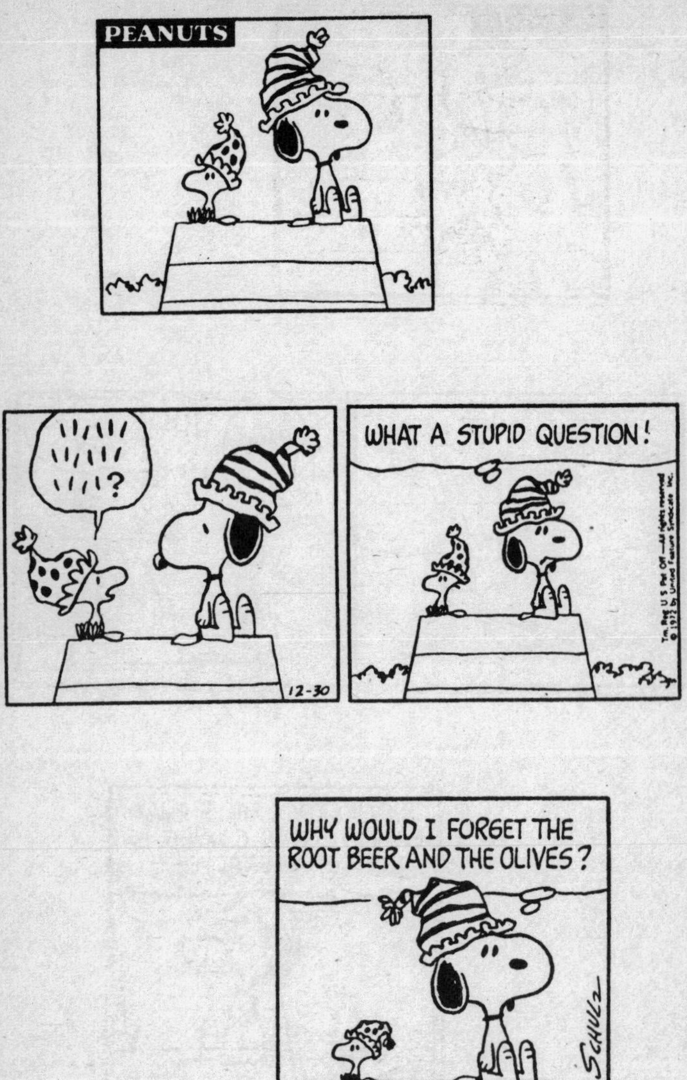
PEANUTS
WHAT A STUPID QUESTION!
Tm. Reg U S Pat Off—All rights reserved © 1972 by United Feature Syndicate Inc.
12-30
WHY WOULD I FORGET THE ROOT BEER AND THE OLIVES?
SCHULZ

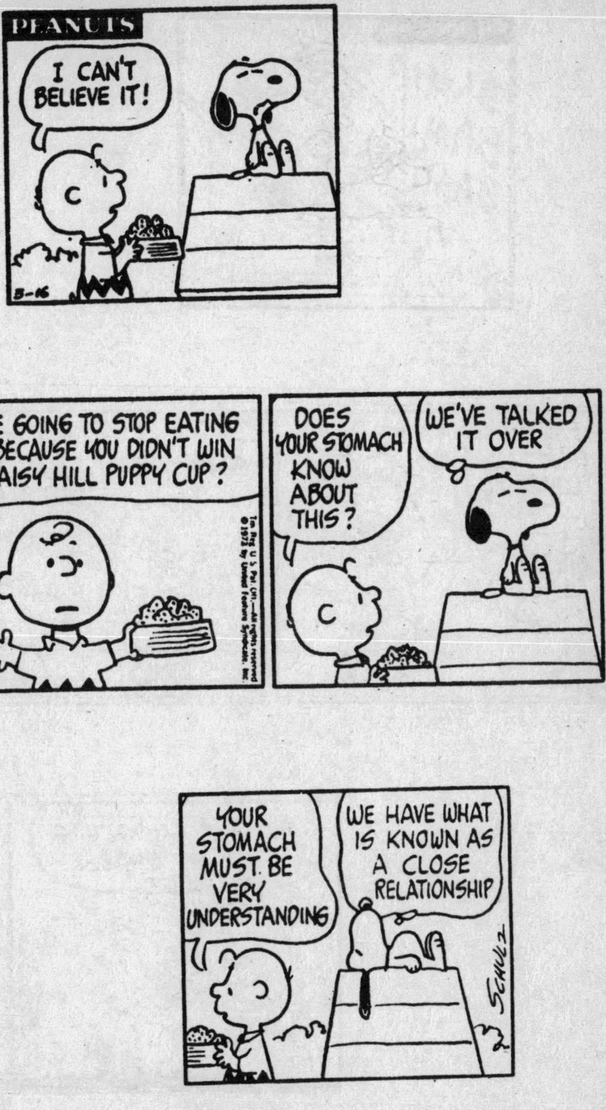
PEANUTS
I CAN'T BELIEVE IT!
3-16
YOU'RE GOING TO STOP EATING JUST BECAUSE YOU DIDN'T WIN THE DAISY HILL PUPPY CUP?
Tm Reg U S Pat. Off.—All rights reserved © 1973 by United Feature Syndicate, Inc.
DOES YOUR STOMACH KNOW ABOUT THIS?
WE'VE TALKED IT OVER
YOUR STOMACH MUST BE VERY UNDERSTANDING
WE HAVE WHAT IS KNOWN AS A CLOSE RELATIONSHIP
SCHULZ

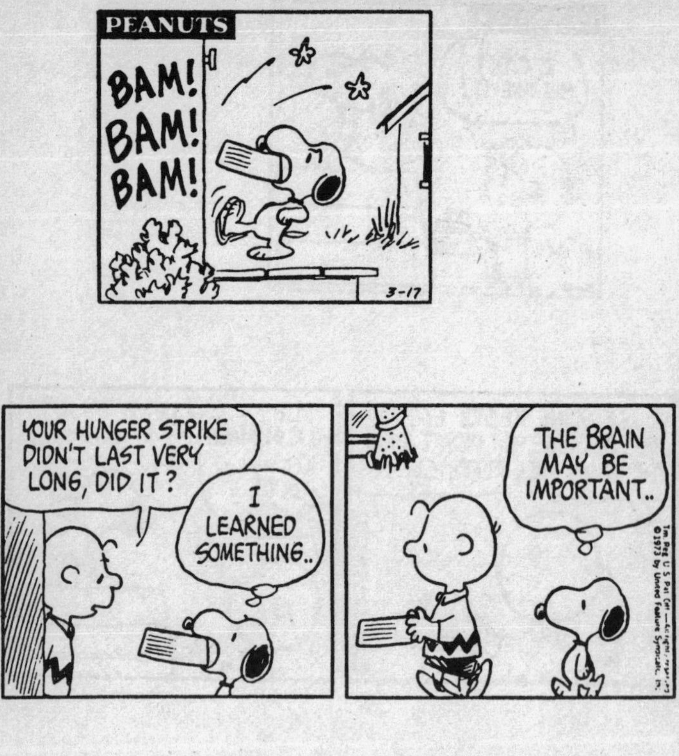
PEANUTS
BAM! BAM! BAM!
3-17
YOUR HUNGER STRIKE DIDN'T LAST VERY LONG, DID IT?
I LEARNED SOMETHING..
THE BRAIN MAY BE IMPORTANT..
..BUT THE STOMACH IS STILL IN CHARGE!
SCHULZ

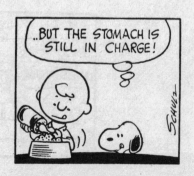

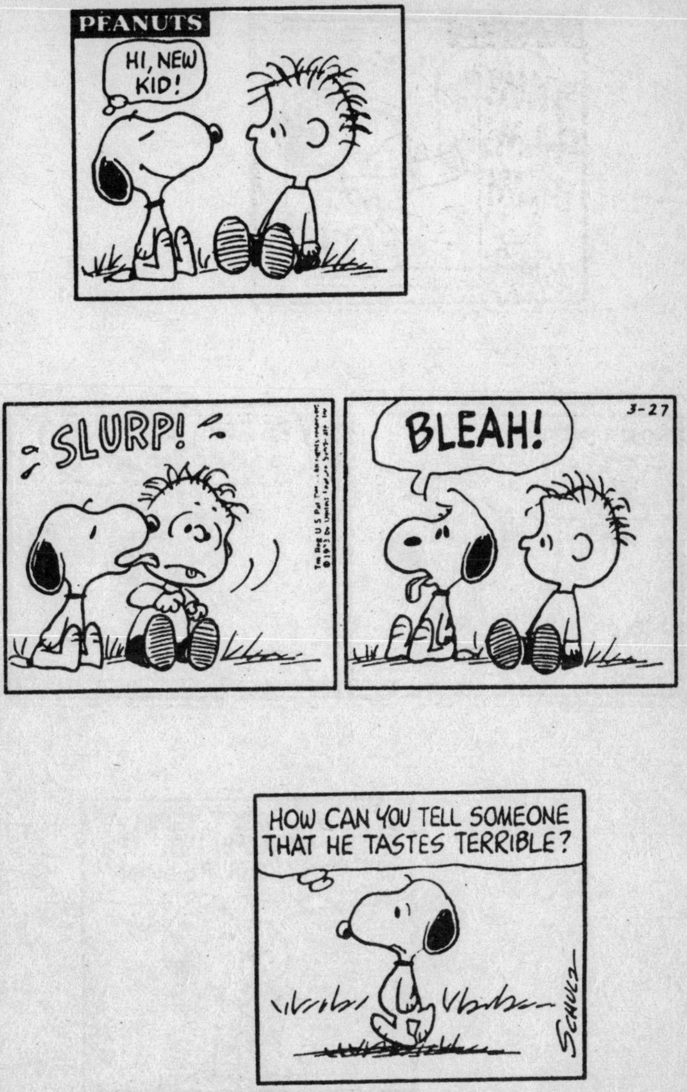
PEANUTS
HI, NEW KID!
SLURP!
3-27
BLEAH!
HOW CAN YOU TELL SOMEONE THAT HE TASTES TERRIBLE?
SCHULZ

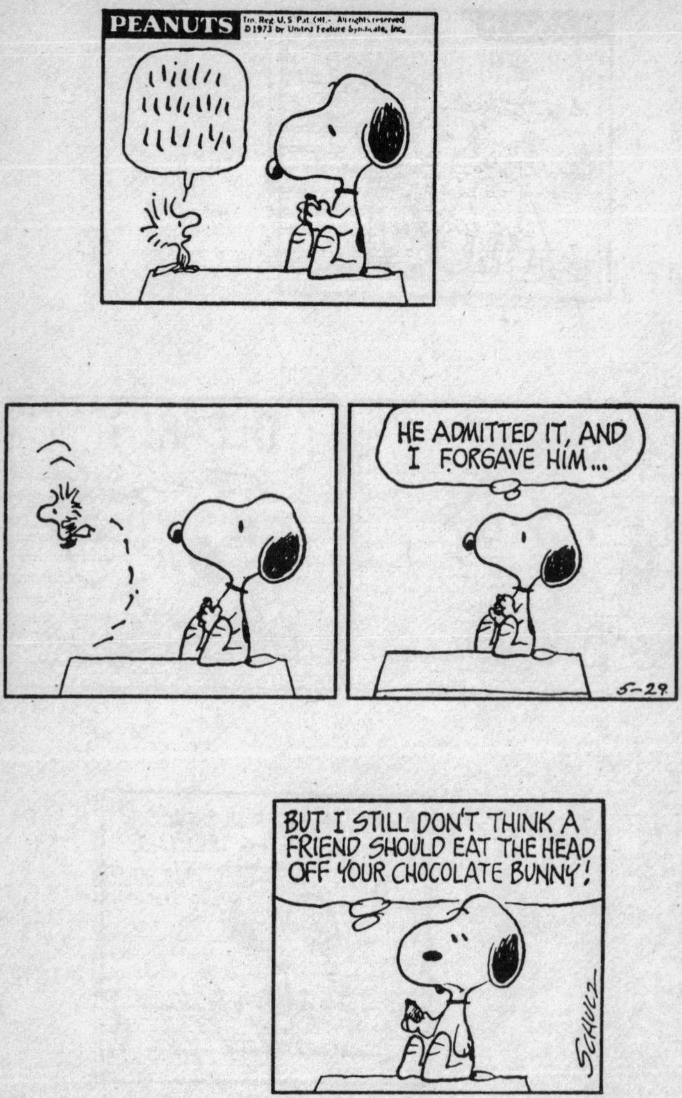
PEANUTS
Tm. Reg. U.S. Pat. Off.- All rights reserved ©1973 by United Feature Syndicate, Inc.
HE ADMITTED IT, AND I FORGAVE HIM...
5-29
BUT I STILL DON'T THINK A FRIEND SHOULD EAT THE HEAD OFF YOUR CHOCOLATE BUNNY!
SCHULZ

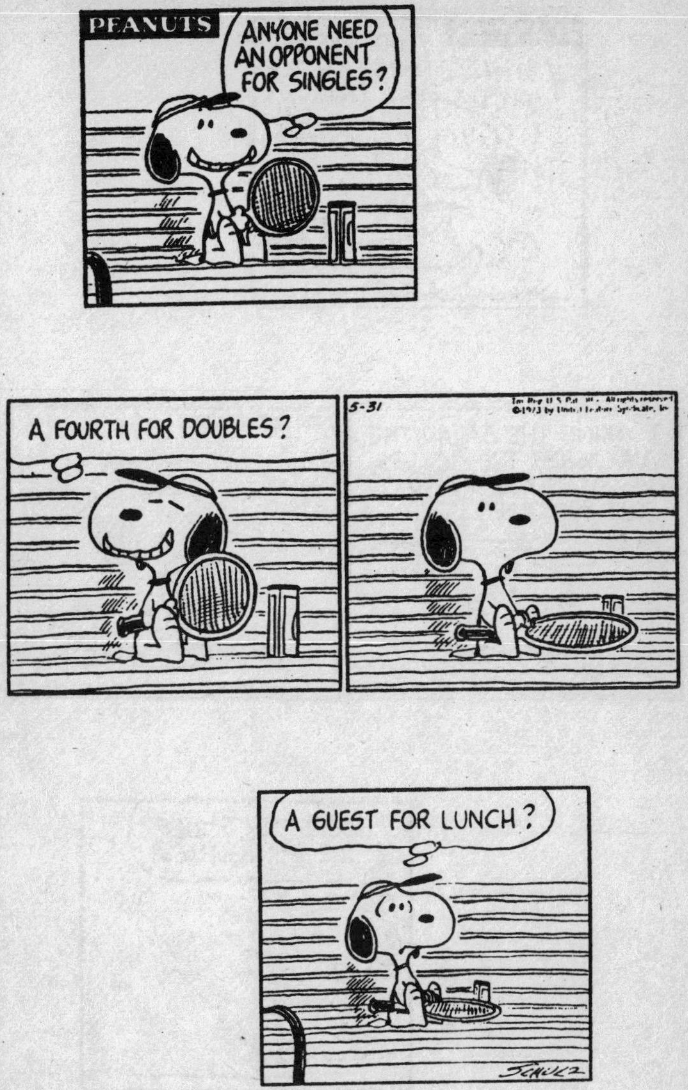
PEANUTS
ANYONE NEED AN OPPONENT FOR SINGLES?
A FOURTH FOR DOUBLES?
5-31
A GUEST FOR LUNCH?
SCHULZ

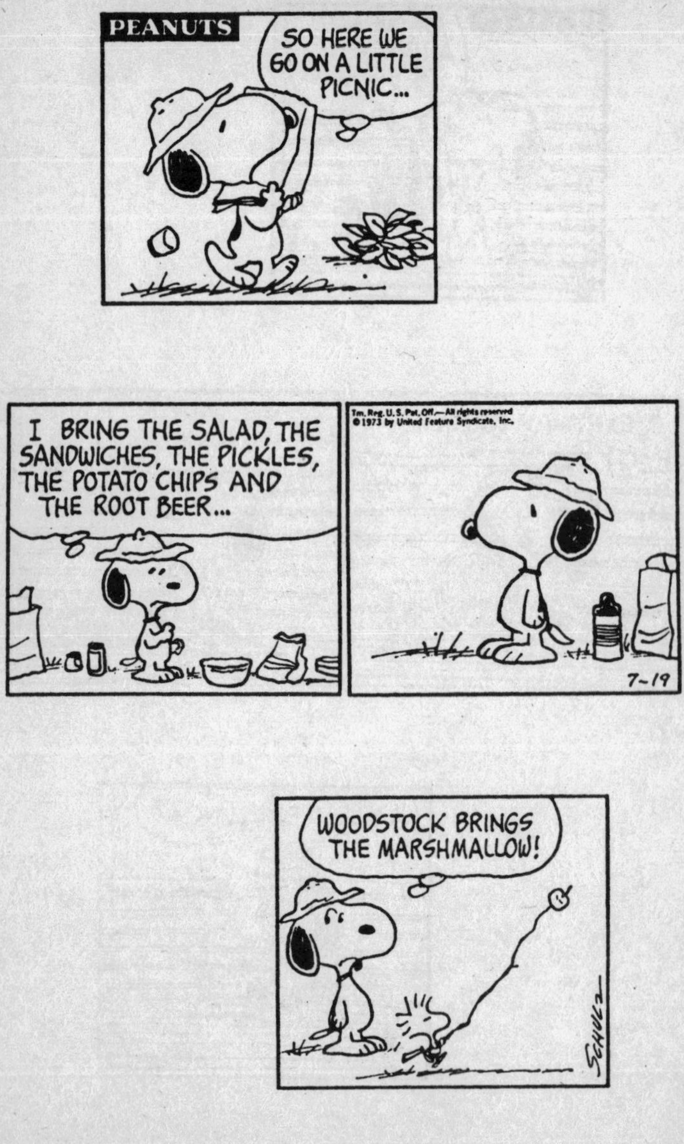
PEANUTS
SO HERE WE GO ON A LITTLE PICNIC...
I BRING THE SALAD, THE SANDWICHES, THE PICKLES, THE POTATO CHIPS AND THE ROOT BEER...
Tm. Reg. U.S. Pat. Off.—All rights reserved ©1973 by United Feature Syndicate, Inc.
7-19
WOODSTOCK BRINGS THE MARSHMALLOW!
SCHULZ

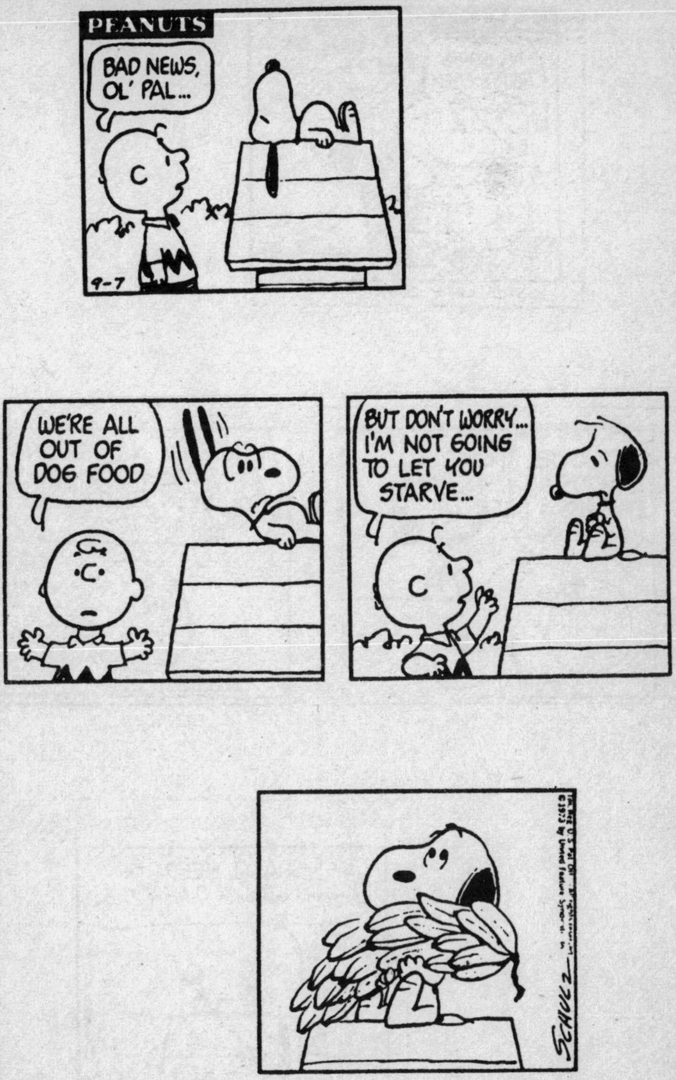
PEANUTS
BAD NEWS, OL' PAL...
9-7
WE'RE ALL OUT OF DOG FOOD
BUT DON'T WORRY... I'M NOT GOING TO LET YOU STARVE...
SCHULZ

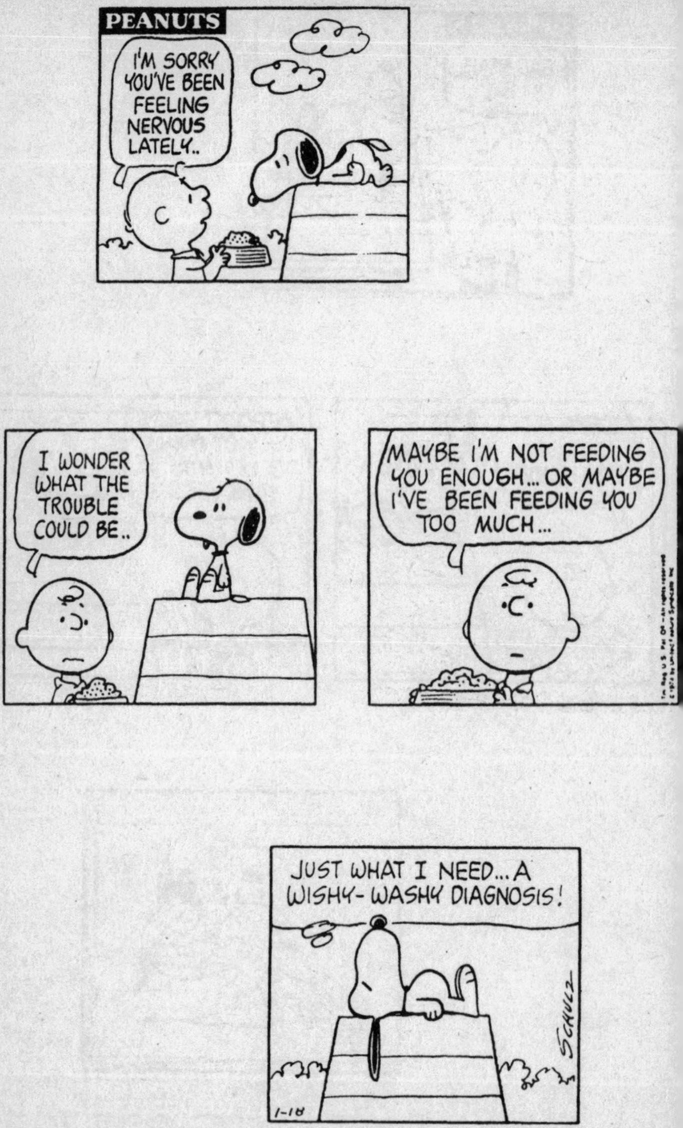
PEANUTS
I'M SORRY YOU'VE BEEN FEELING NERVOUS LATELY..
I WONDER WHAT THE TROUBLE COULD BE..
MAYBE I'M NOT FEEDING YOU ENOUGH... OR MAYBE I'VE BEEN FEEDING YOU TOO MUCH...
JUST WHAT I NEED... A WISHY-WASHY DIAGNOSIS!
SCHULZ
1-18

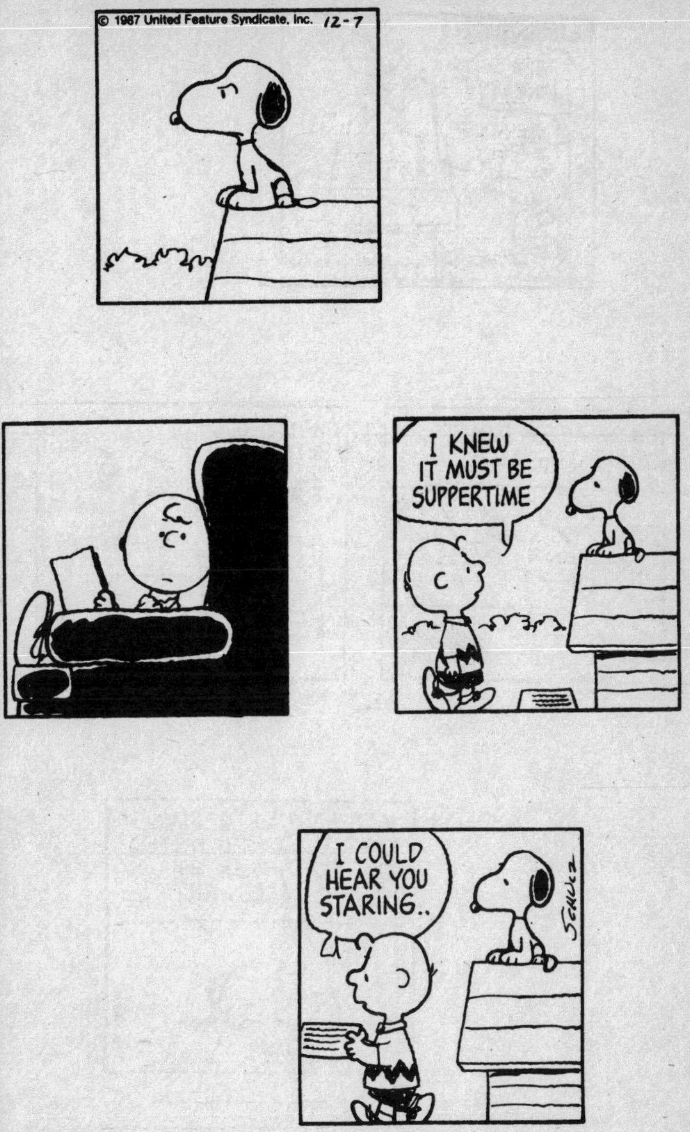
© 1987 United Feature Syndicate, Inc. 12-7
I KNEW IT MUST BE SUPPERTIME
I COULD HEAR YOU STARING..
SCHULZ

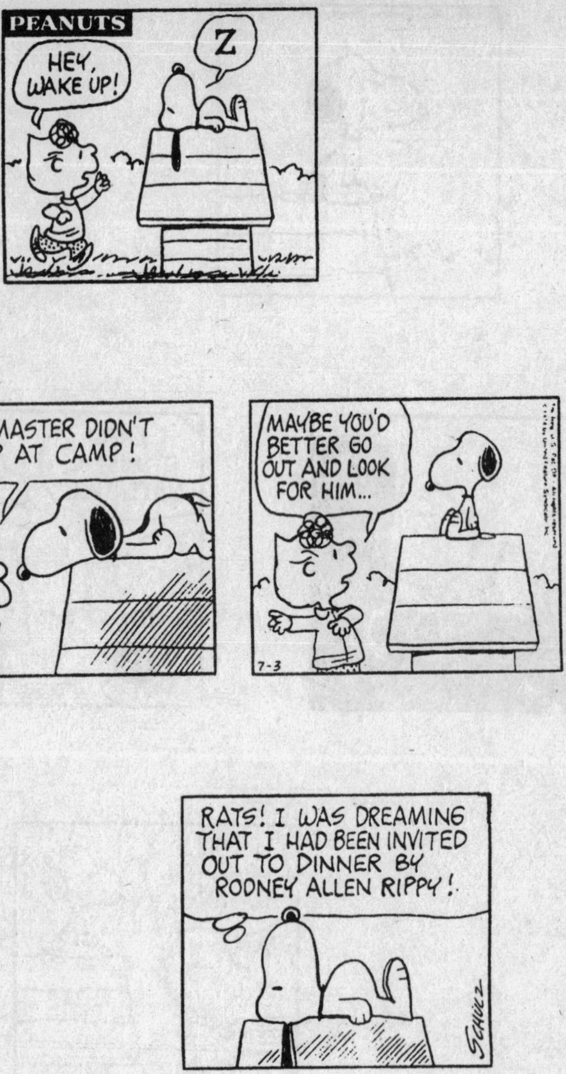
PEANUTS
HEY, WAKE UP!
Z
YOUR MASTER DIDN'T SHOW UP AT CAMP!
MAYBE YOU'D BETTER GO OUT AND LOOK FOR HIM...
7-3
RATS! I WAS DREAMING THAT I HAD BEEN INVITED OUT TO DINNER BY RODNEY ALLEN RIPPY!
SCHULZ

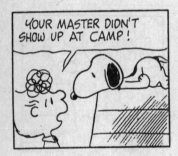

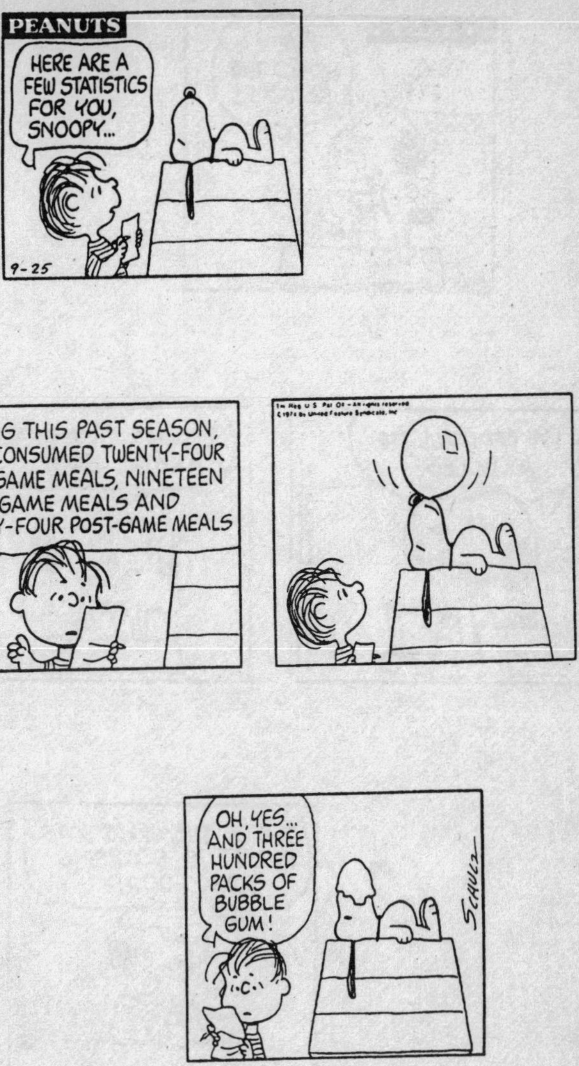
PEANUTS
HERE ARE A FEW STATISTICS FOR YOU, SNOOPY...
9-25
DURING THIS PAST SEASON, YOU CONSUMED TWENTY-FOUR PRE-GAME MEALS, NINETEEN MID-GAME MEALS AND FIFTY-FOUR POST-GAME MEALS
OH, YES... AND THREE HUNDRED PACKS OF BUBBLE GUM!
SCHULZ

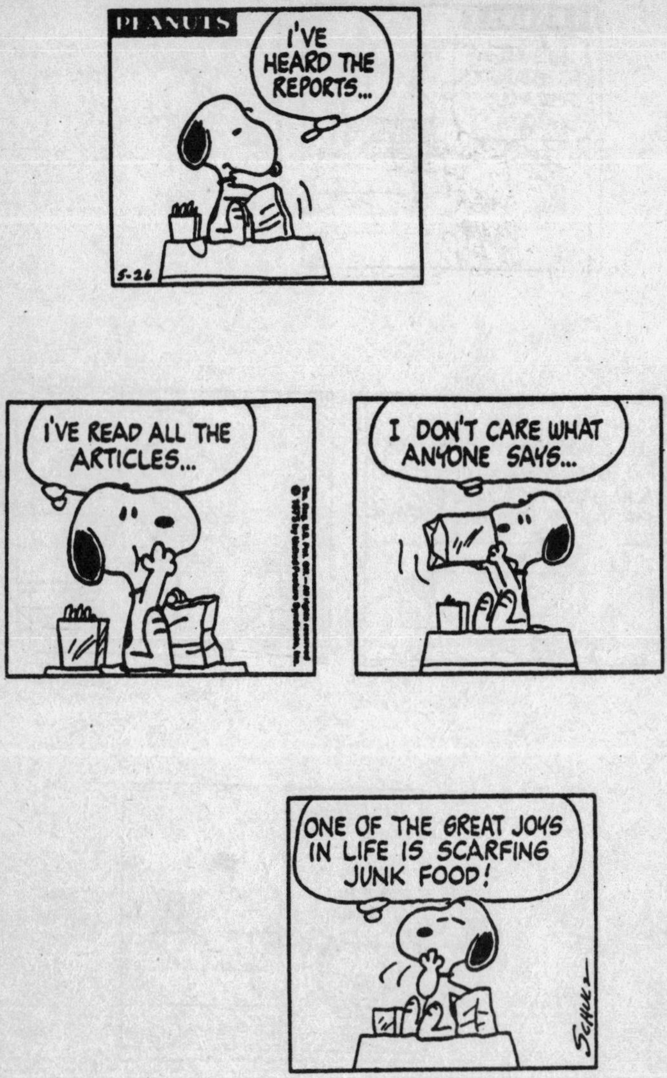
PEANUTS
I'VE HEARD THE REPORTS...
5-26
I'VE READ ALL THE ARTICLES...
I DON'T CARE WHAT ANYONE SAYS...
ONE OF THE GREAT JOYS IN LIFE IS SCARFING JUNK FOOD!
SCHULZ

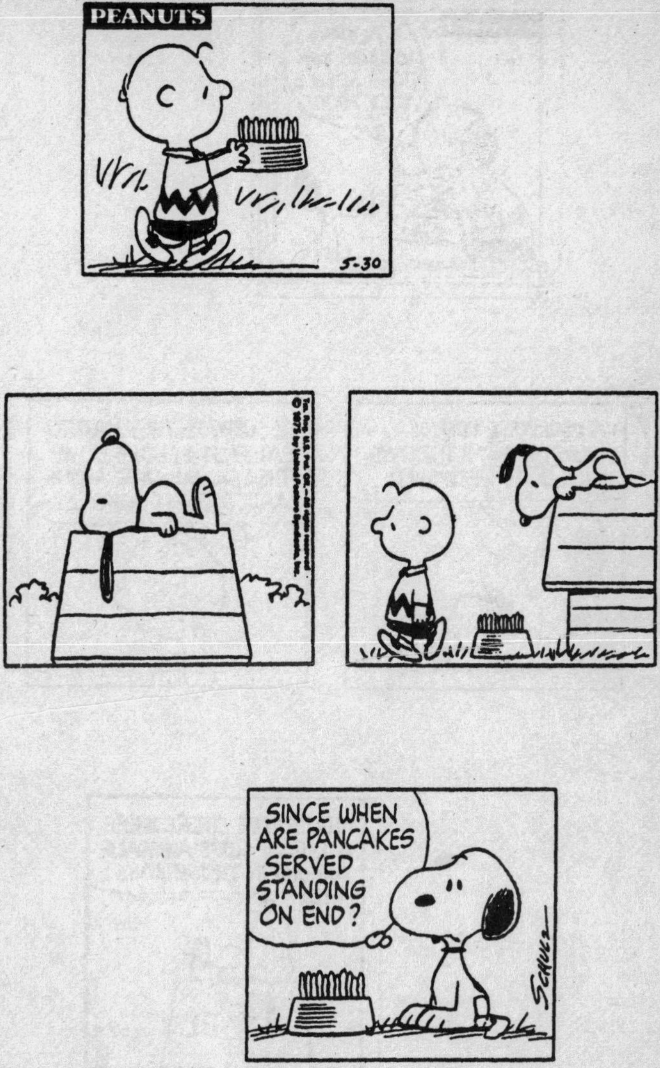
PEANUTS
5-30
SINCE WHEN ARE PANCAKES SERVED STANDING ON END?
SCHULZ

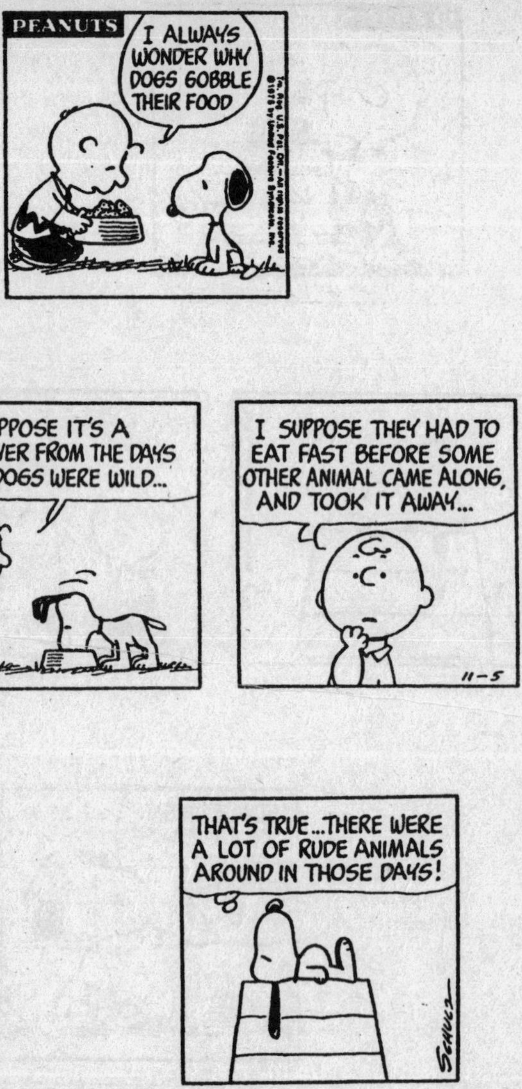
PEANUTS
I ALWAYS WONDER WHY DOGS GOBBLE THEIR FOOD
I SUPPOSE IT'S A HOLDOVER FROM THE DAYS WHEN DOGS WERE WILD...
I SUPPOSE THEY HAD TO EAT FAST BEFORE SOME OTHER ANIMAL CAME ALONG, AND TOOK IT AWAY...
11-5
THAT'S TRUE...THERE WERE A LOT OF RUDE ANIMALS AROUND IN THOSE DAYS!
SCHULZ

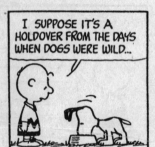

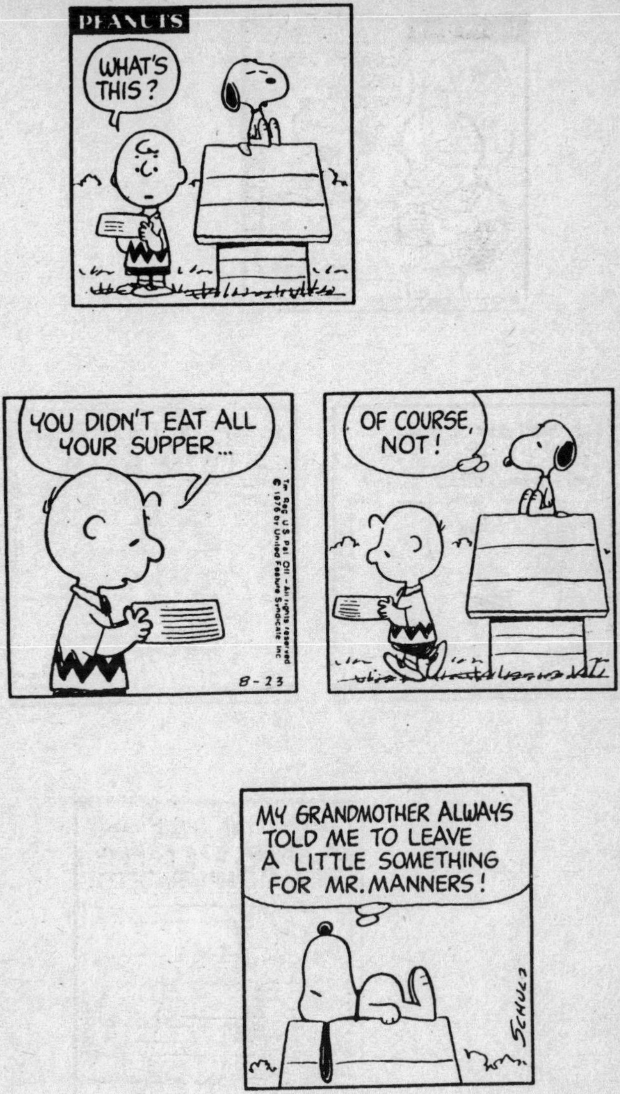
PEANUTS
WHAT'S THIS?
YOU DIDN'T EAT ALL YOUR SUPPER...
Tm Reg U.S. Pat Off — All rights reserved © 1976 by United Feature Syndicate Inc
8-23
OF COURSE, NOT!
MY GRANDMOTHER ALWAYS TOLD ME TO LEAVE A LITTLE SOMETHING FOR MR. MANNERS!
SCHULZ

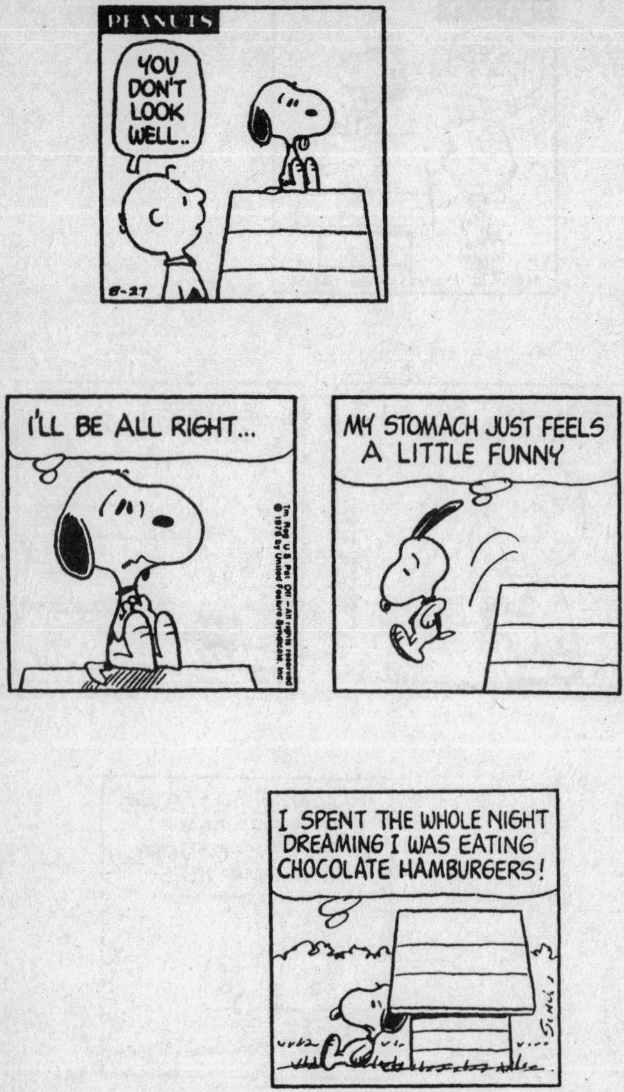
PEANUTS
YOU DON'T LOOK WELL..
8-27
I'LL BE ALL RIGHT...
MY STOMACH JUST FEELS A LITTLE FUNNY
I SPENT THE WHOLE NIGHT DREAMING I WAS EATING CHOCOLATE HAMBURGERS!

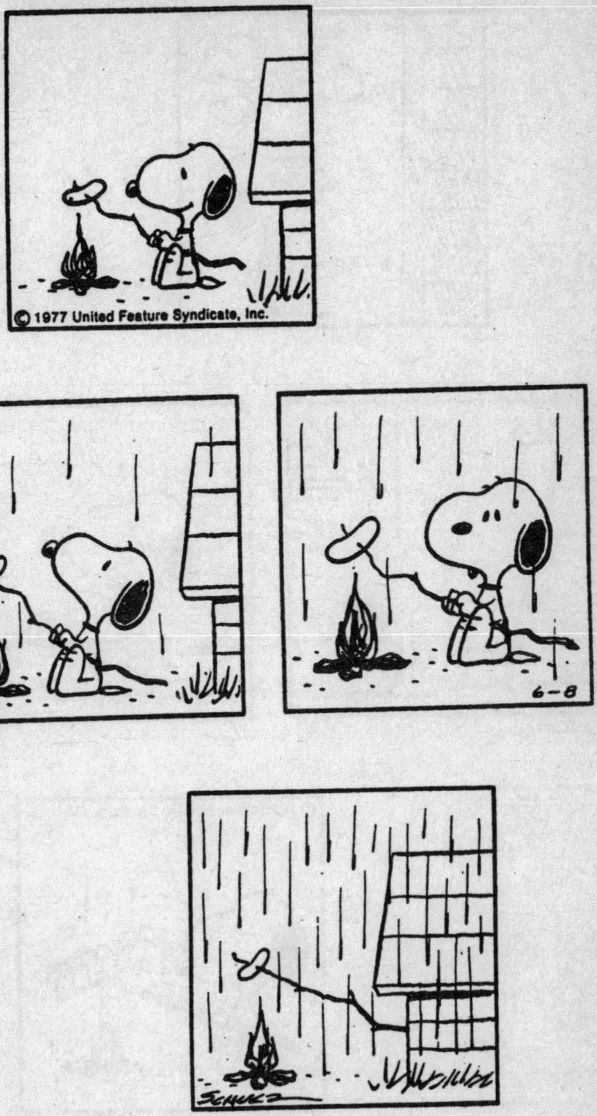
© 1977 United Feature Syndicate, Inc.
6-8

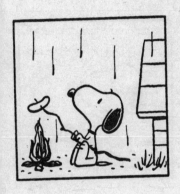

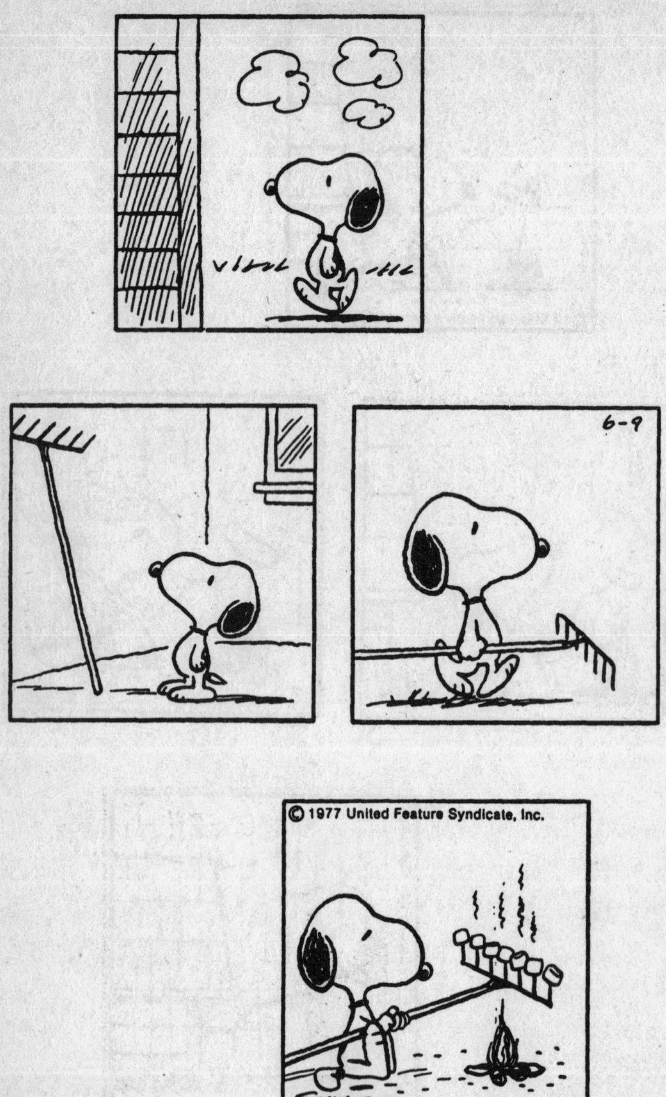
6-9
© 1977 United Feature Syndicate, Inc.
SCHULZ

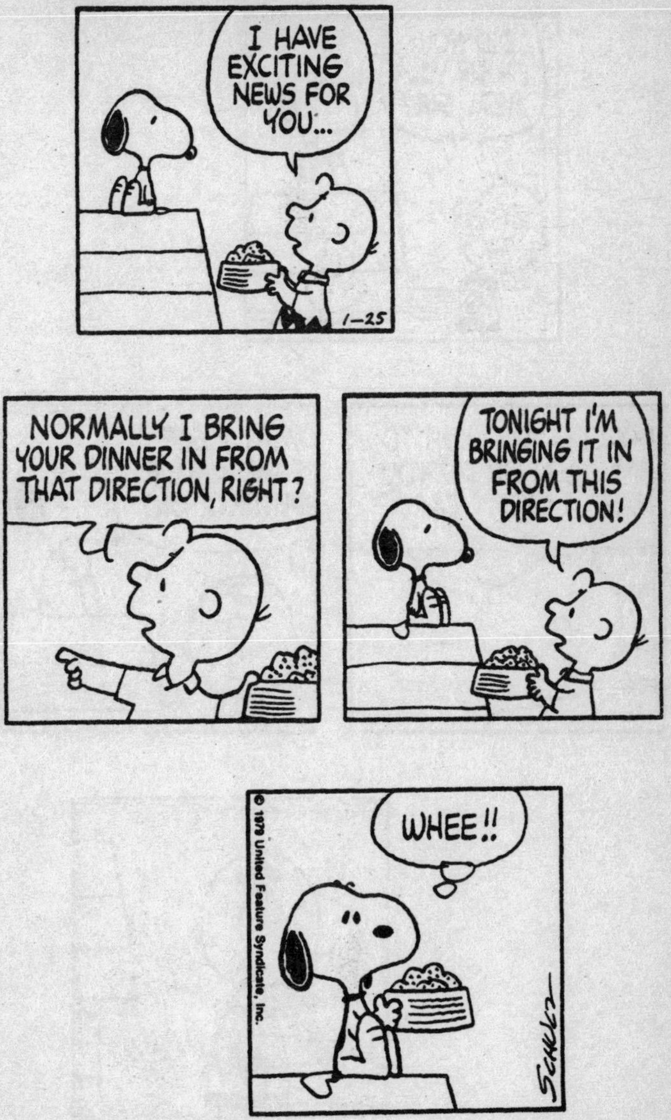
I HAVE EXCITING NEWS FOR YOU...
1-25
NORMALLY I BRING YOUR DINNER IN FROM THAT DIRECTION, RIGHT?
TONIGHT I'M BRINGING IT IN FROM THIS DIRECTION!
WHEE!!
© 1978 United Feature Syndicate, Inc.
SCHULZ

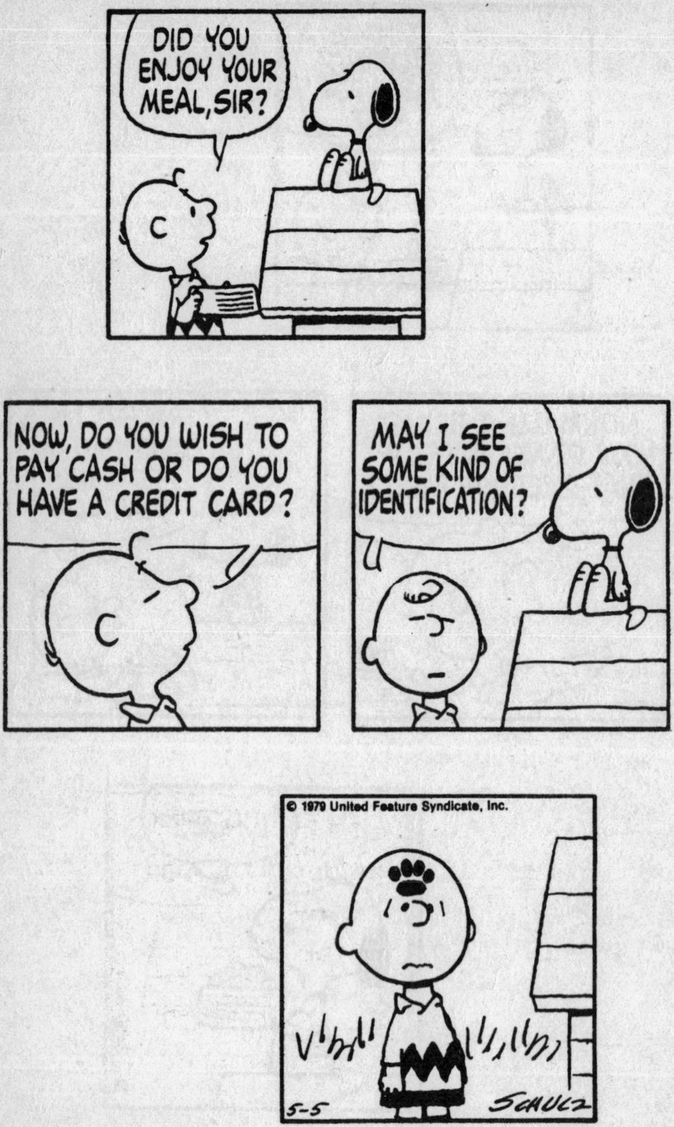
DID YOU ENJOY YOUR MEAL, SIR?
NOW, DO YOU WISH TO PAY CASH OR DO YOU HAVE A CREDIT CARD?
MAY I SEE SOME KIND OF IDENTIFICATION?
© 1979 United Feature Syndicate, Inc.
5-5
SCHULZ

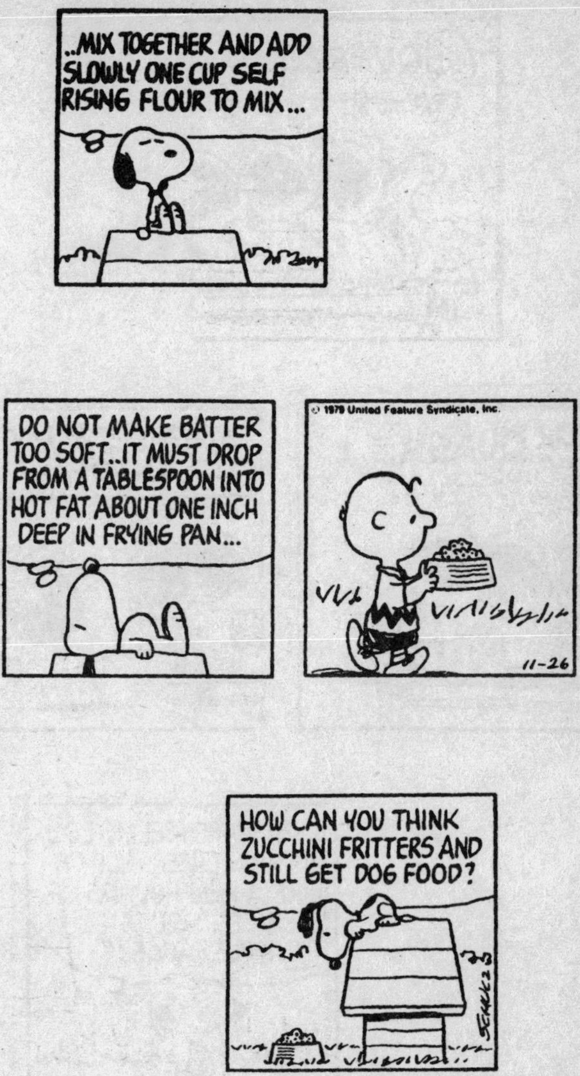
..MIX TOGETHER AND ADD SLOWLY ONE CUP SELF RISING FLOUR TO MIX...
DO NOT MAKE BATTER TOO SOFT..IT MUST DROP FROM A TABLESPOON INTO HOT FAT ABOUT ONE INCH DEEP IN FRYING PAN...
© 1979 United Feature Syndicate, Inc.
11-26
HOW CAN YOU THINK ZUCCHINI FRITTERS AND STILL GET DOG FOOD?

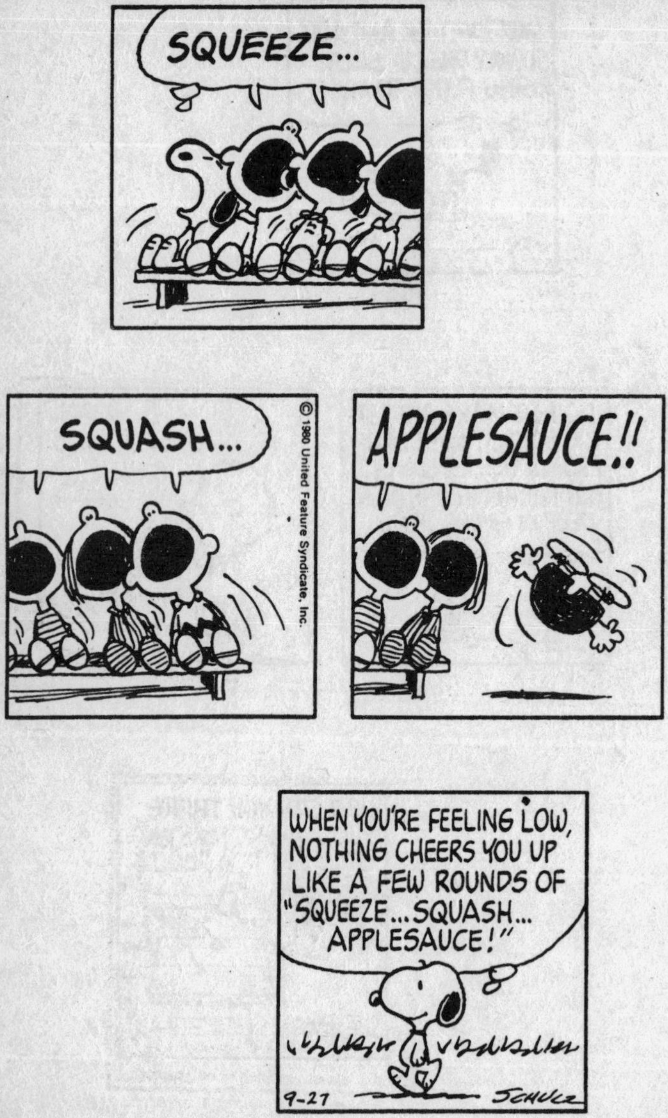
SQUEEZE...
SQUASH...
© 1980 United Feature Syndicate, Inc.
APPLESAUCE!!
WHEN YOU'RE FEELING LOW, NOTHING CHEERS YOU UP LIKE A FEW ROUNDS OF "SQUEEZE...SQUASH... APPLESAUCE!"
9-27
SCHULZ

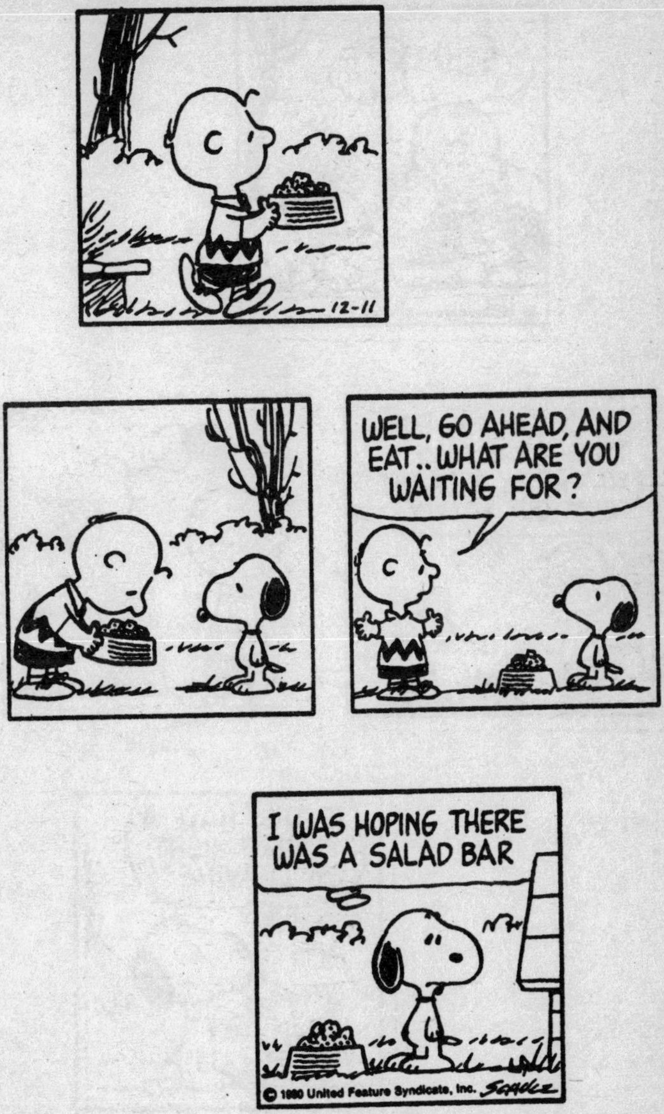
12-11
WELL, GO AHEAD, AND EAT.. WHAT ARE YOU WAITING FOR?
I WAS HOPING THERE WAS A SALAD BAR
© 1980 United Feature Syndicate, Inc.

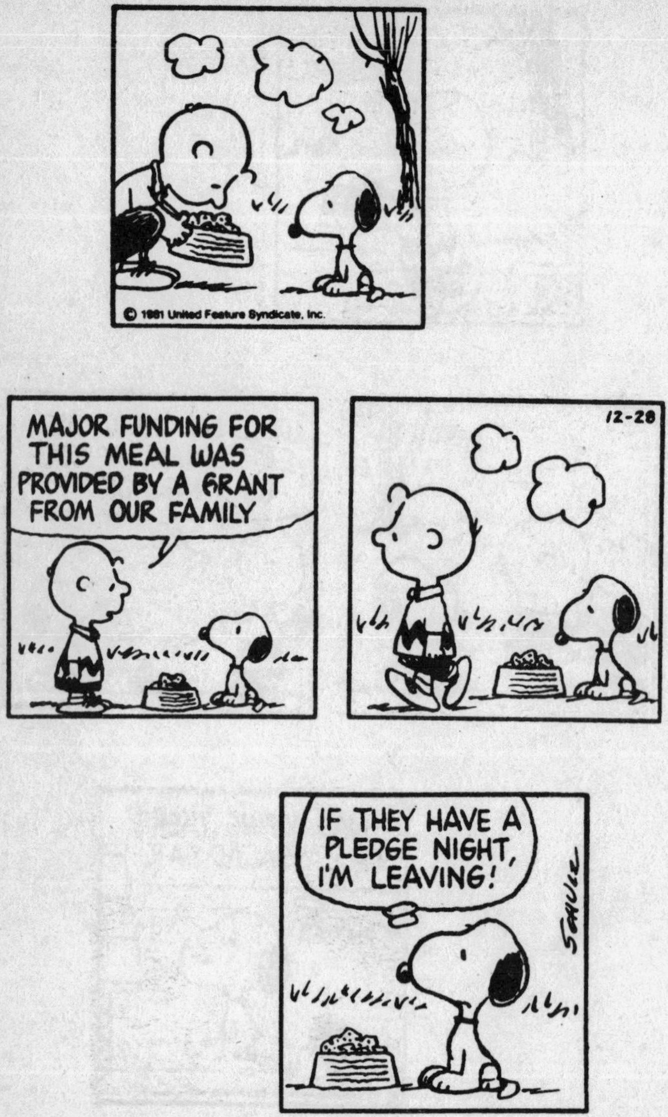
© 1981 United Feature Syndicate, Inc.
MAJOR FUNDING FOR THIS MEAL WAS PROVIDED BY A GRANT FROM OUR FAMILY
12-28
IF THEY HAVE A PLEDGE NIGHT, I'M LEAVING!
SCHULZ

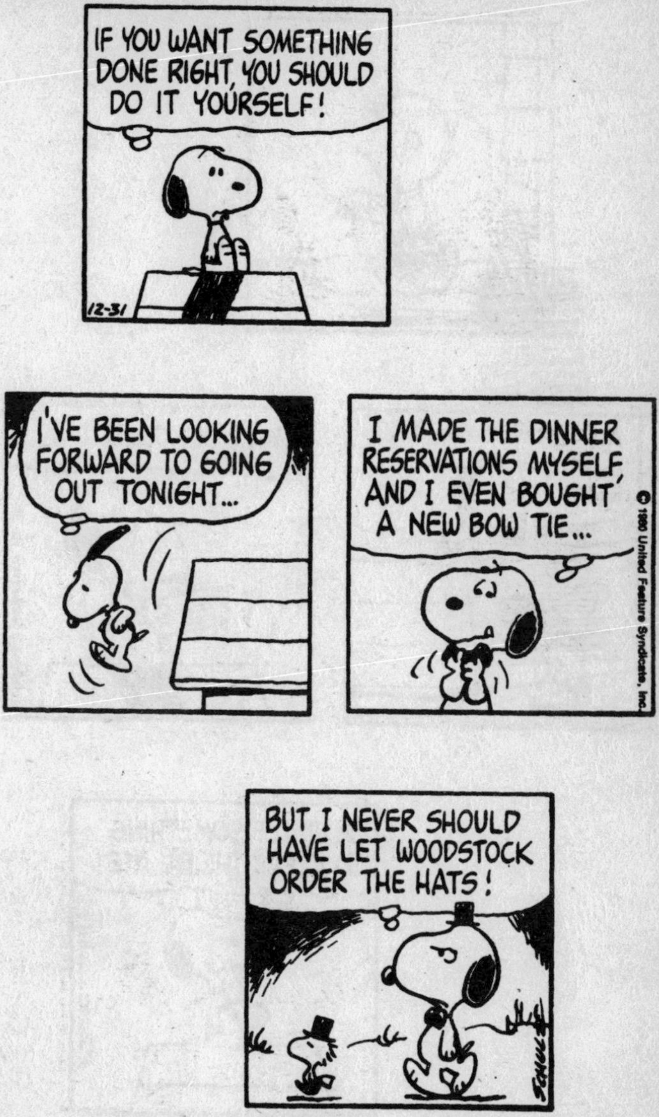
IF YOU WANT SOMETHING DONE RIGHT, YOU SHOULD DO IT YOURSELF!
12-31
I'VE BEEN LOOKING FORWARD TO GOING OUT TONIGHT...
I MADE THE DINNER RESERVATIONS MYSELF, AND I EVEN BOUGHT A NEW BOW TIE...
© 1980 United Feature Syndicate, Inc.
BUT I NEVER SHOULD HAVE LET WOODSTOCK ORDER THE HATS!
SCHULZ

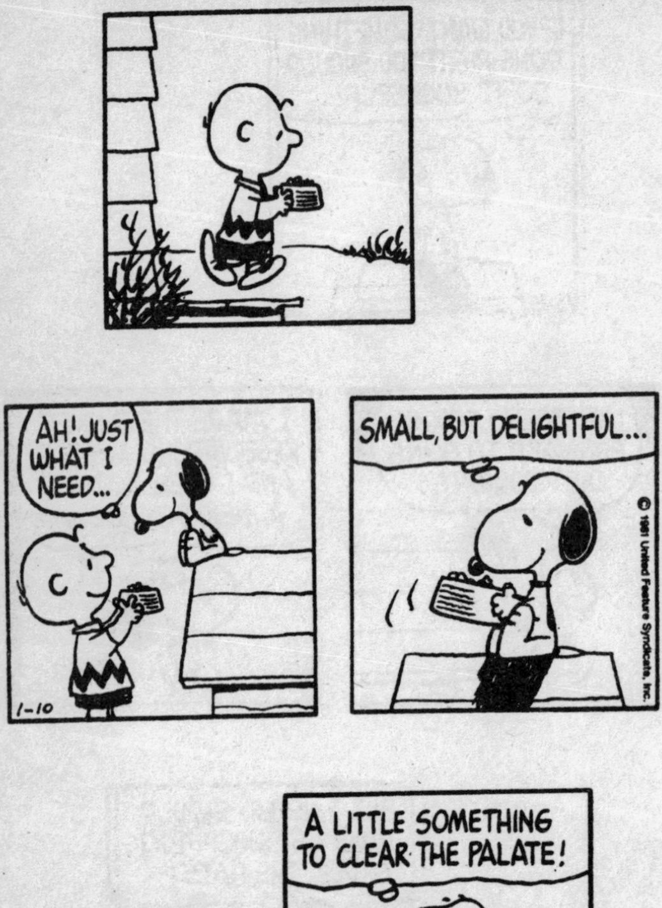
AH! JUST WHAT I NEED...
1-10
SMALL, BUT DELIGHTFUL...
© 1981 United Feature Syndicate, Inc.
A LITTLE SOMETHING TO CLEAR THE PALATE!
SCHULZ

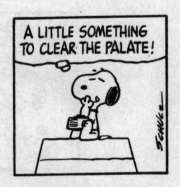

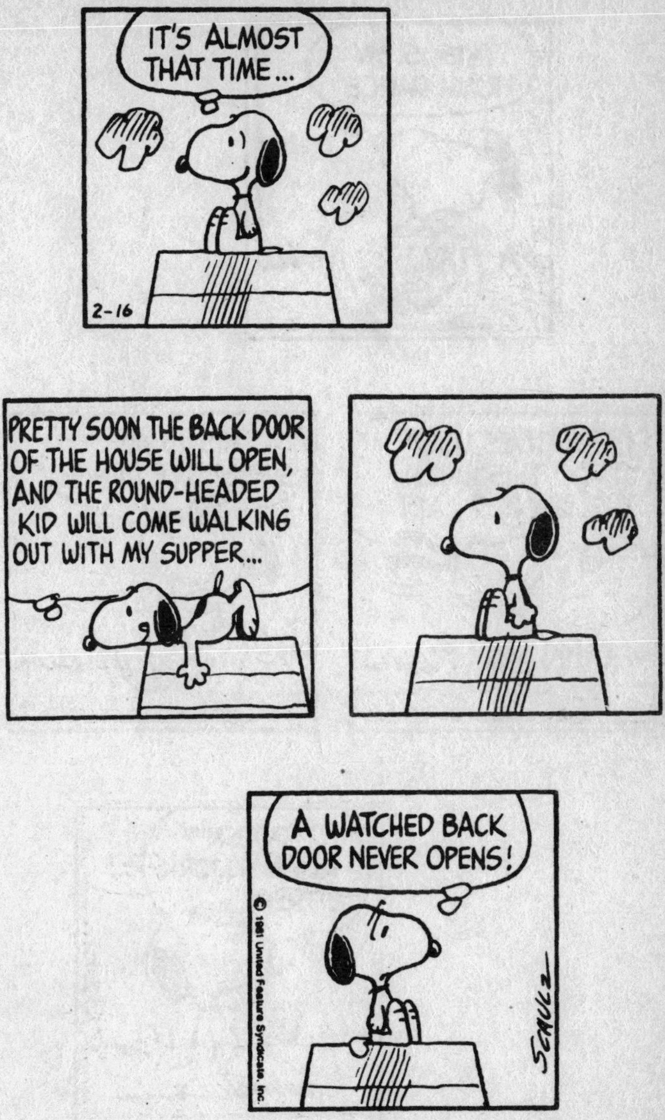
IT'S ALMOST THAT TIME...
2-16
PRETTY SOON THE BACK DOOR OF THE HOUSE WILL OPEN, AND THE ROUND-HEADED KID WILL COME WALKING OUT WITH MY SUPPER...
A WATCHED BACK DOOR NEVER OPENS!
© 1981 United Feature Syndicate, Inc.
SCHULZ

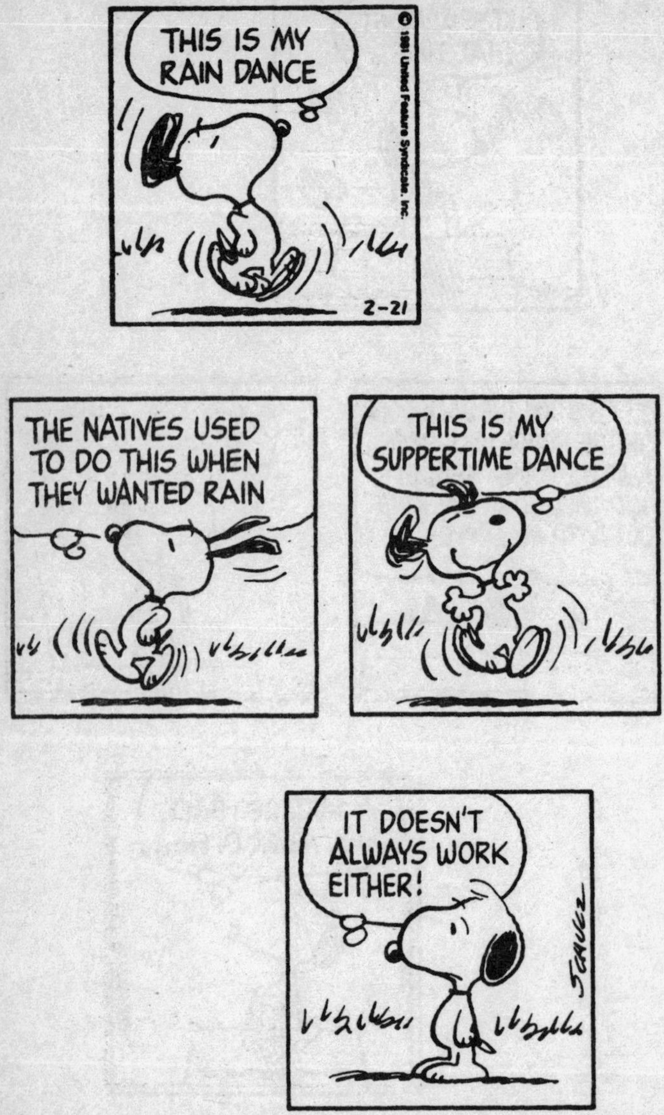
THIS IS MY RAIN DANCE
© 1981 United Feature Syndicate, Inc.
2-21
THE NATIVES USED TO DO THIS WHEN THEY WANTED RAIN
THIS IS MY SUPPERTIME DANCE
IT DOESN'T ALWAYS WORK EITHER!

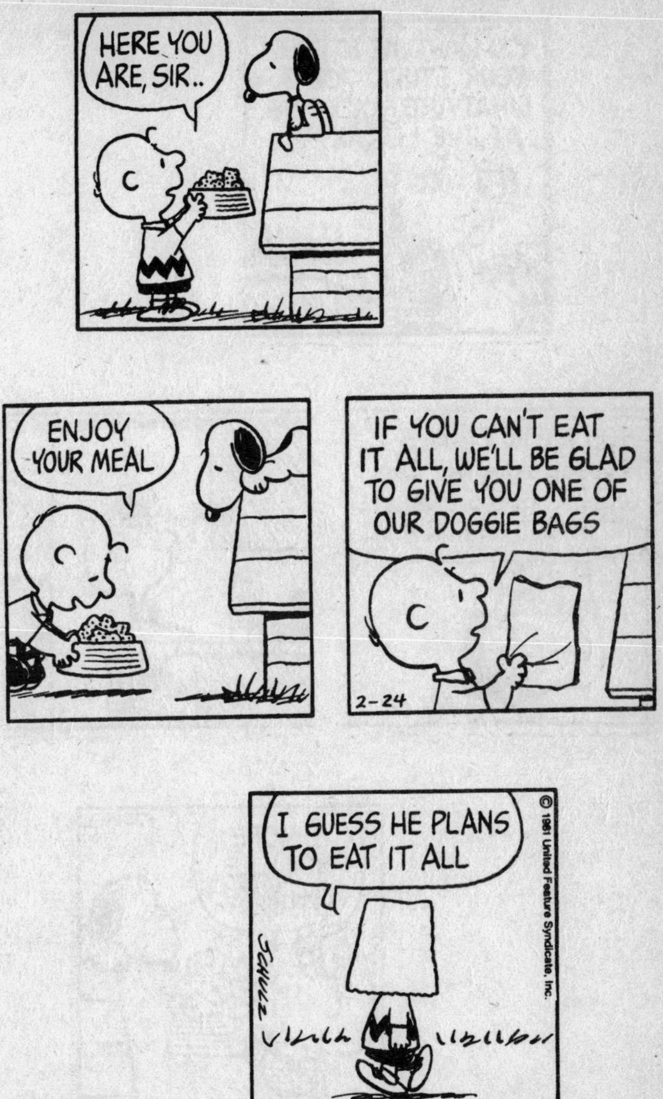
HERE YOU ARE, SIR..
ENJOY YOUR MEAL
IF YOU CAN'T EAT IT ALL, WE'LL BE GLAD TO GIVE YOU ONE OF OUR DOGGIE BAGS
2-24
I GUESS HE PLANS TO EAT IT ALL
SCHULZ
© 1981 United Feature Syndicate, Inc.

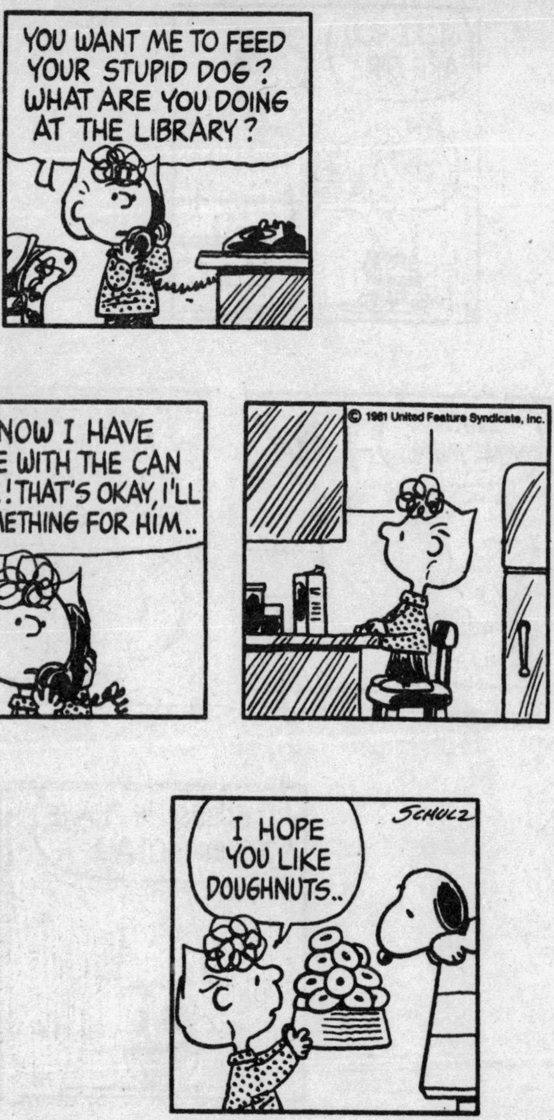
YOU WANT ME TO FEED YOUR STUPID DOG? WHAT ARE YOU DOING AT THE LIBRARY?
YOU KNOW I HAVE TROUBLE WITH THE CAN OPENER! THAT'S OKAY, I'LL FIND SOMETHING FOR HIM..
2-25
© 1981 United Feature Syndicate, Inc.
SCHULZ
I HOPE YOU LIKE DOUGHNUTS..

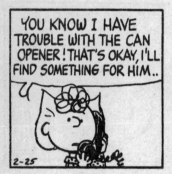

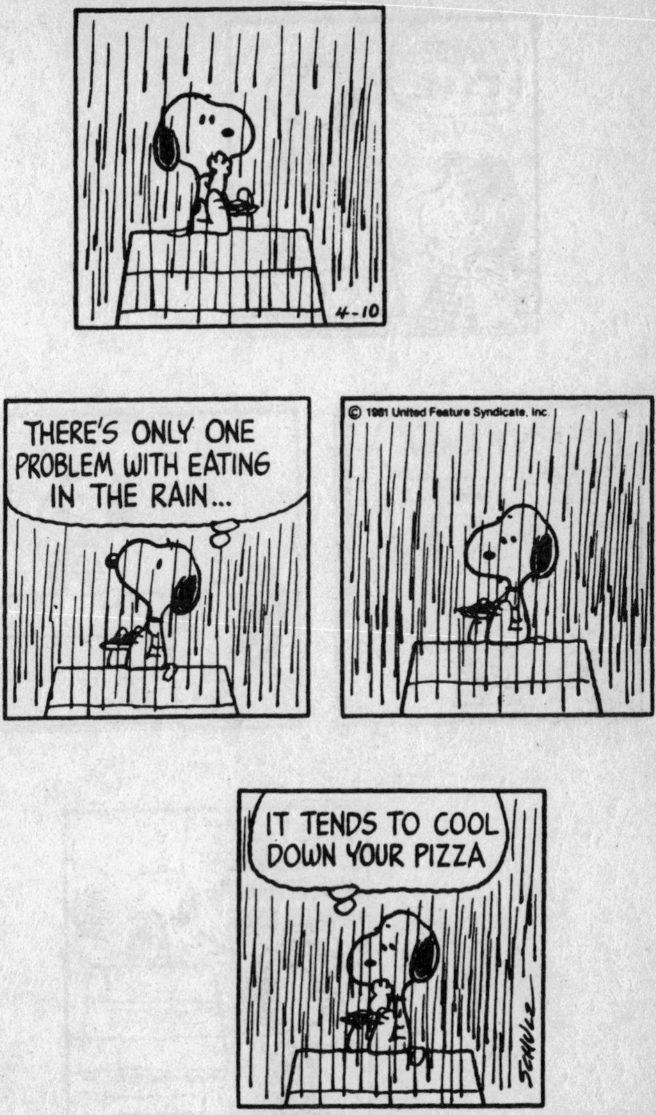
4-10
THERE'S ONLY ONE PROBLEM WITH EATING IN THE RAIN...
© 1981 United Feature Syndicate, Inc.
IT TENDS TO COOL DOWN YOUR PIZZA
SCHULZ

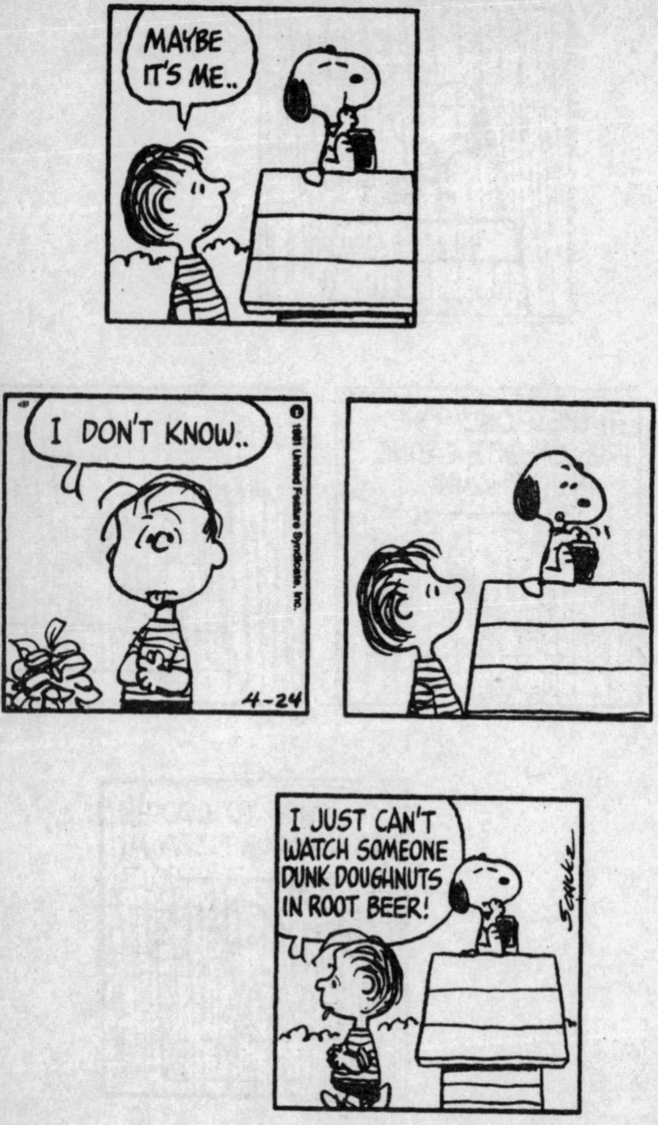
MAYBE IT'S ME..
I DON'T KNOW..
© 1981 United Feature Syndicate, Inc.
4-24
I JUST CAN'T WATCH SOMEONE DUNK DOUGHNUTS IN ROOT BEER!
SCHULZ

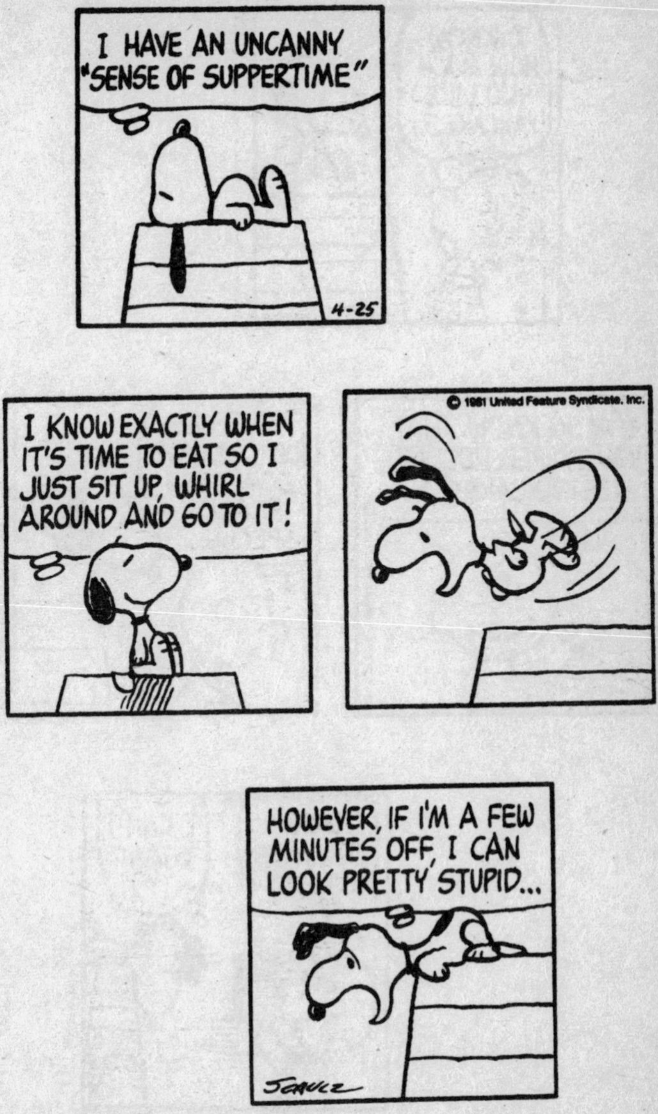
I HAVE AN UNCANNY "SENSE OF SUPPERTIME"
4-25
I KNOW EXACTLY WHEN IT'S TIME TO EAT SO I JUST SIT UP, WHIRL AROUND AND GO TO IT!
© 1981 United Feature Syndicate, Inc.
HOWEVER, IF I'M A FEW MINUTES OFF, I CAN LOOK PRETTY STUPID...
SCHULZ

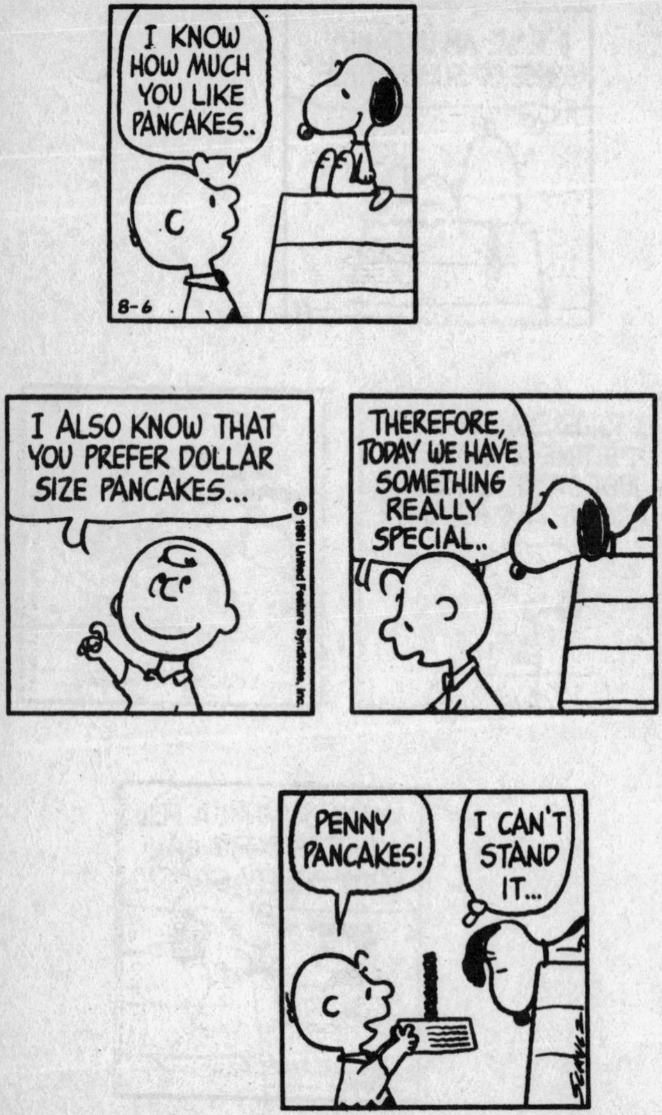
I KNOW HOW MUCH YOU LIKE PANCAKES..
8-6
I ALSO KNOW THAT YOU PREFER DOLLAR SIZE PANCAKES...
© 1981 United Feature Syndicate, Inc.
THEREFORE, TODAY WE HAVE SOMETHING REALLY SPECIAL..
PENNY PANCAKES!
I CAN'T STAND IT...
SCHULZ

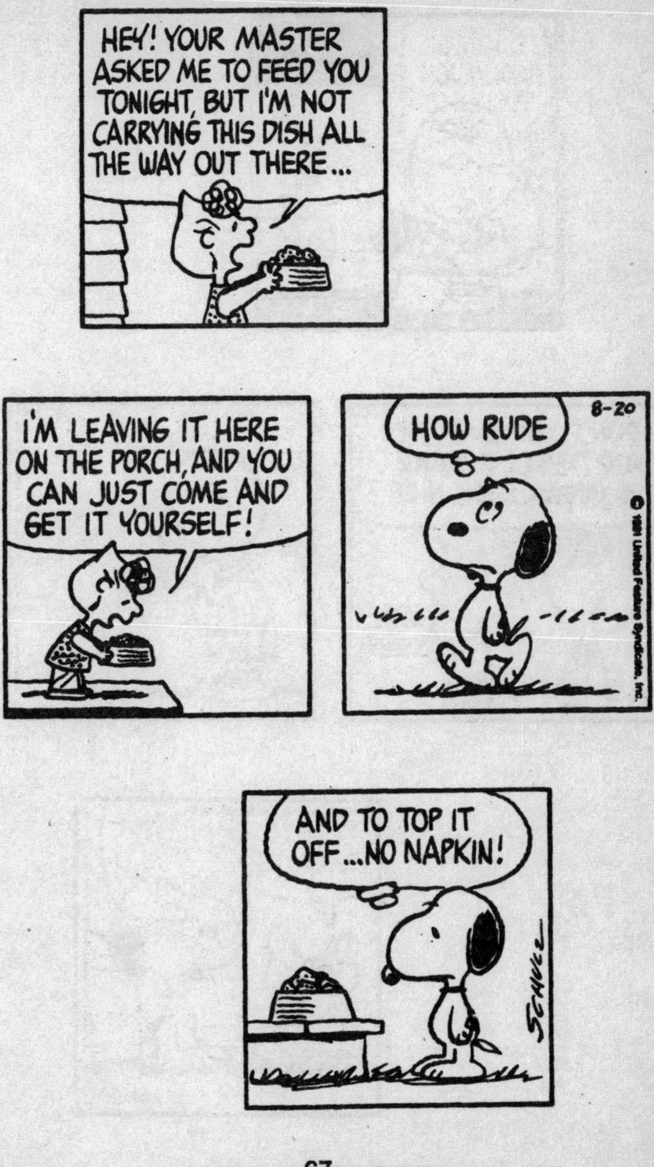
HEY! YOUR MASTER ASKED ME TO FEED YOU TONIGHT, BUT I'M NOT CARRYING THIS DISH ALL THE WAY OUT THERE...
I'M LEAVING IT HERE ON THE PORCH, AND YOU CAN JUST COME AND GET IT YOURSELF!
8-20
HOW RUDE
© 1981 United Feature Syndicate, Inc.
AND TO TOP IT OFF...NO NAPKIN!
SCHULZ

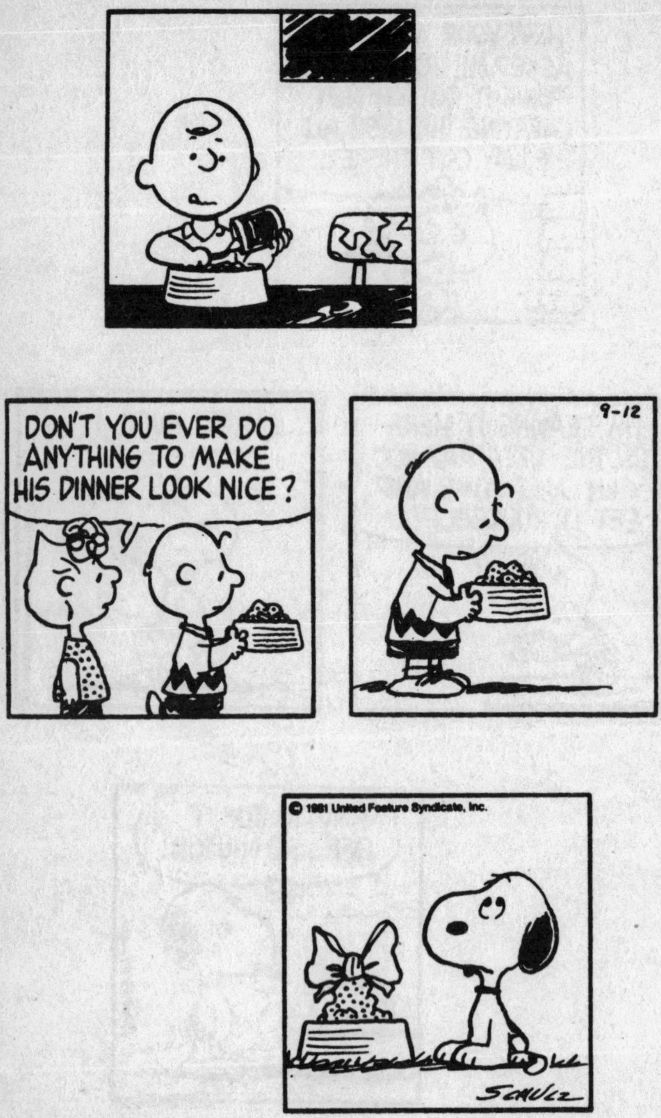
DON'T YOU EVER DO ANYTHING TO MAKE HIS DINNER LOOK NICE?
9-12
© 1981 United Feature Syndicate, Inc.
SCHULZ

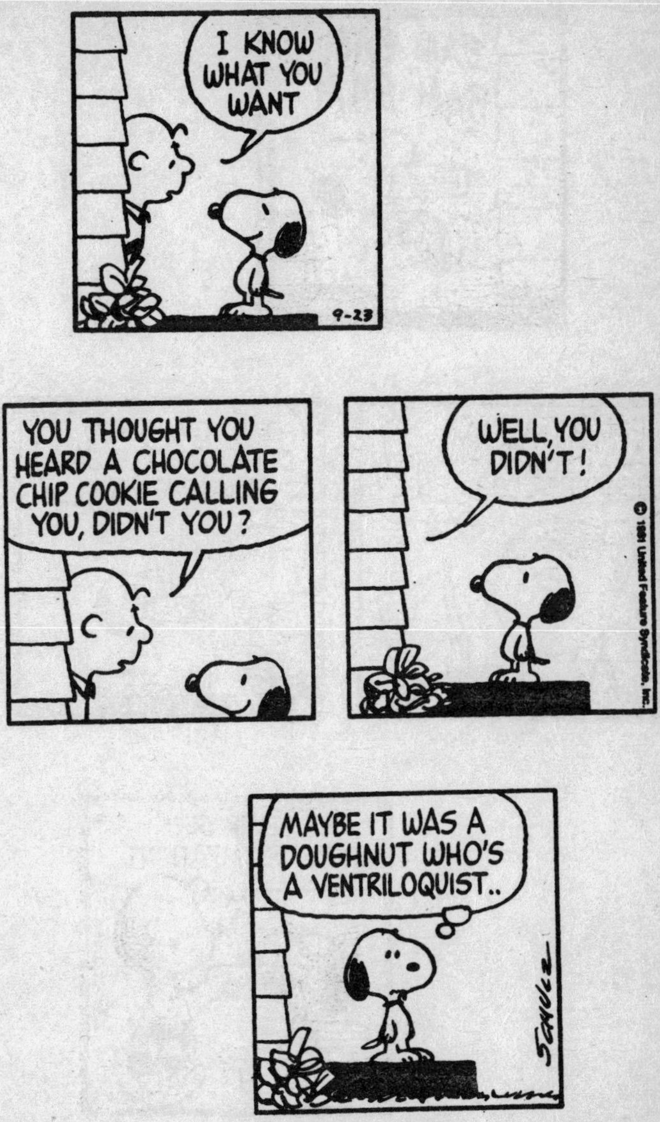
I KNOW WHAT YOU WANT
9-23
YOU THOUGHT YOU HEARD A CHOCOLATE CHIP COOKIE CALLING YOU, DIDN'T YOU?
WELL, YOU DIDN'T!
© 1981 United Feature Syndicate, Inc.
MAYBE IT WAS A DOUGHNUT WHO'S A VENTRILOQUIST..
SCHULZ

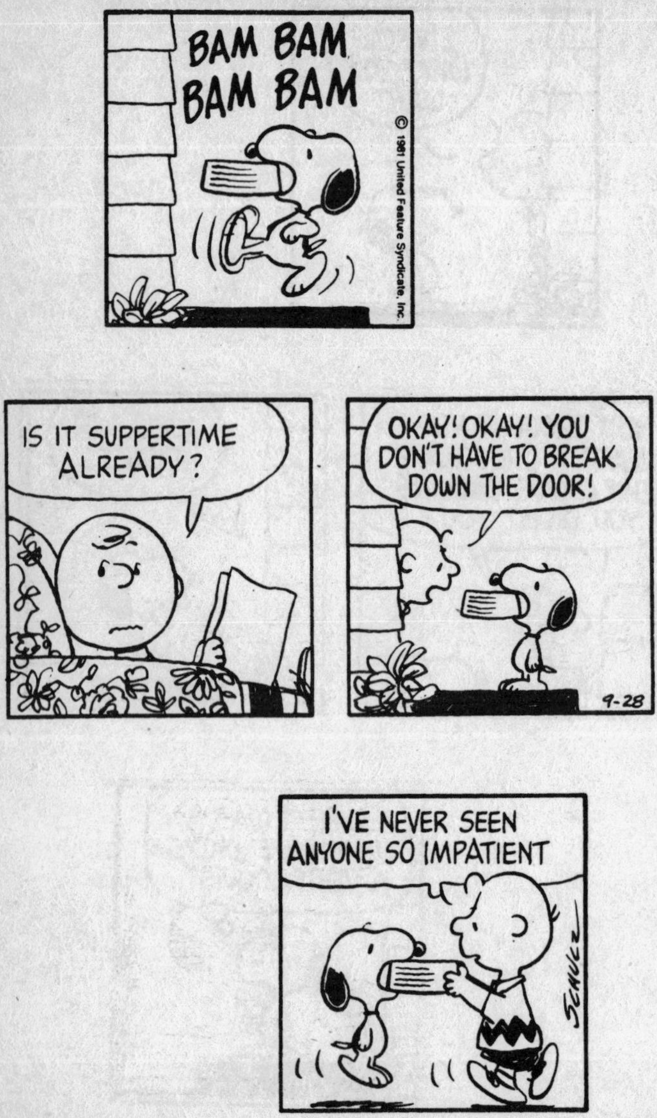
BAM BAM
BAM BAM
© 1981 United Feature Syndicate, Inc.
IS IT SUPPERTIME ALREADY?
OKAY! OKAY! YOU DON'T HAVE TO BREAK DOWN THE DOOR!
9-28
I'VE NEVER SEEN ANYONE SO IMPATIENT
SCHULZ

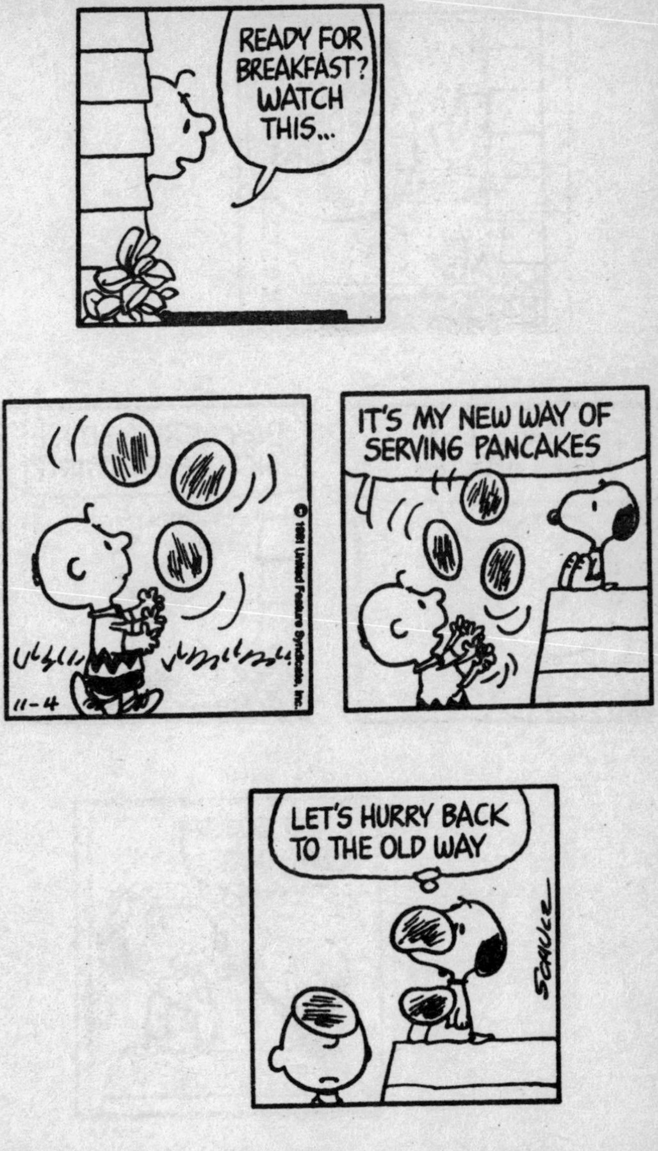
READY FOR BREAKFAST? WATCH THIS...
© 1981 United Feature Syndicate, Inc.
11-4
IT'S MY NEW WAY OF SERVING PANCAKES
LET'S HURRY BACK TO THE OLD WAY
SCHULZ

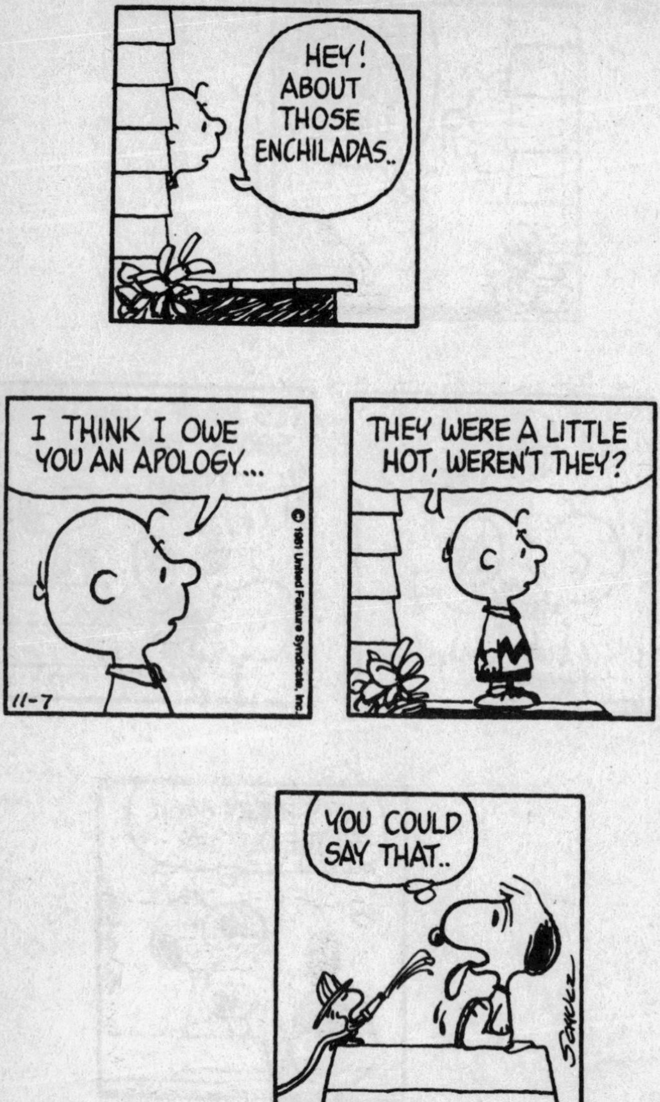
HEY! ABOUT THOSE ENCHILADAS..
I THINK I OWE YOU AN APOLOGY...
11-7
© 1981 United Feature Syndicate, Inc.
THEY WERE A LITTLE HOT, WEREN'T THEY?
YOU COULD SAY THAT..
SCHULZ

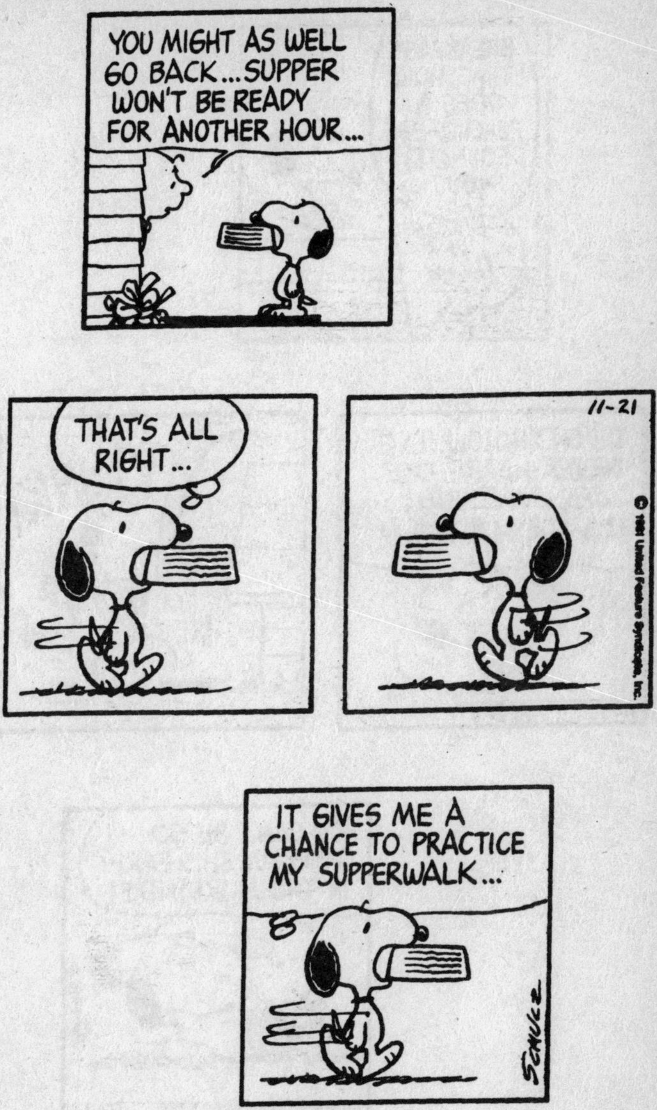
YOU MIGHT AS WELL GO BACK...SUPPER WON'T BE READY FOR ANOTHER HOUR...
THAT'S ALL RIGHT...
11-21
© 1981 United Feature Syndicate, Inc.
IT GIVES ME A CHANCE TO PRACTICE MY SUPPERWALK...
SCHULZ

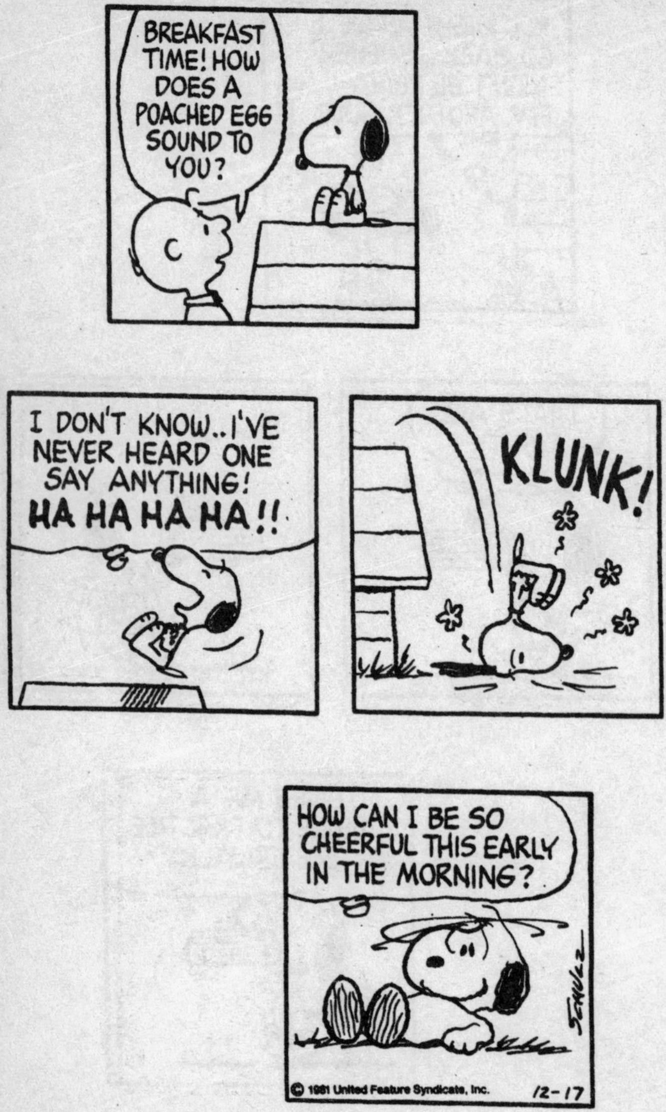
BREAKFAST TIME! HOW DOES A POACHED EGG SOUND TO YOU?
I DON'T KNOW.. I'VE NEVER HEARD ONE SAY ANYTHING! HA HA HA HA!!
KLUNK!
HOW CAN I BE SO CHEERFUL THIS EARLY IN THE MORNING?
SCHULZ
© 1981 United Feature Syndicate, Inc.
12-17

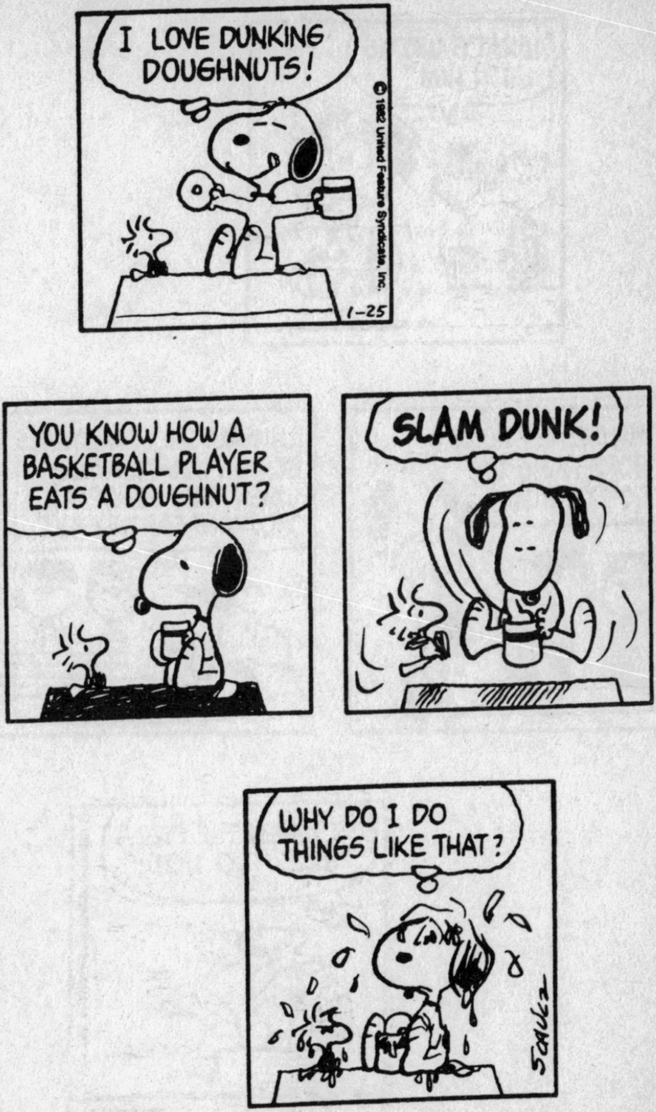
I LOVE DUNKING DOUGHNUTS!
© 1982 United Feature Syndicate, Inc.
1-25
YOU KNOW HOW A BASKETBALL PLAYER EATS A DOUGHNUT?
SLAM DUNK!
WHY DO I DO THINGS LIKE THAT?
SCHULZ

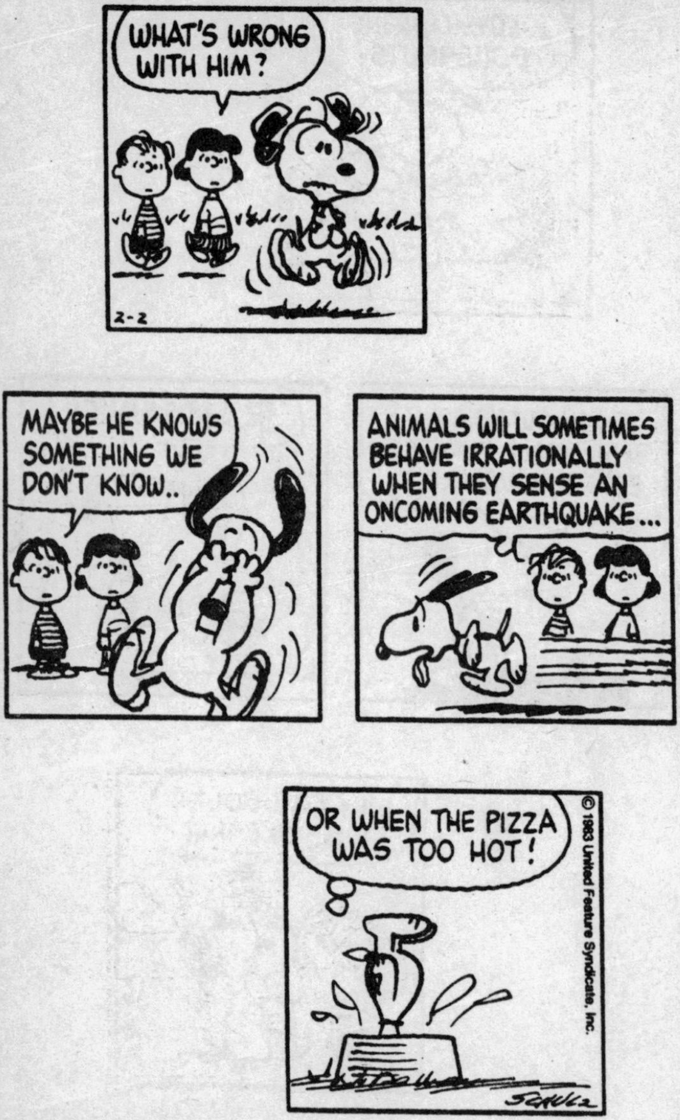
WHAT'S WRONG WITH HIM?
2-2
MAYBE HE KNOWS SOMETHING WE DON'T KNOW..
ANIMALS WILL SOMETIMES BEHAVE IRRATIONALLY WHEN THEY SENSE AN ONCOMING EARTHQUAKE...
OR WHEN THE PIZZA WAS TOO HOT!
SCHULZ

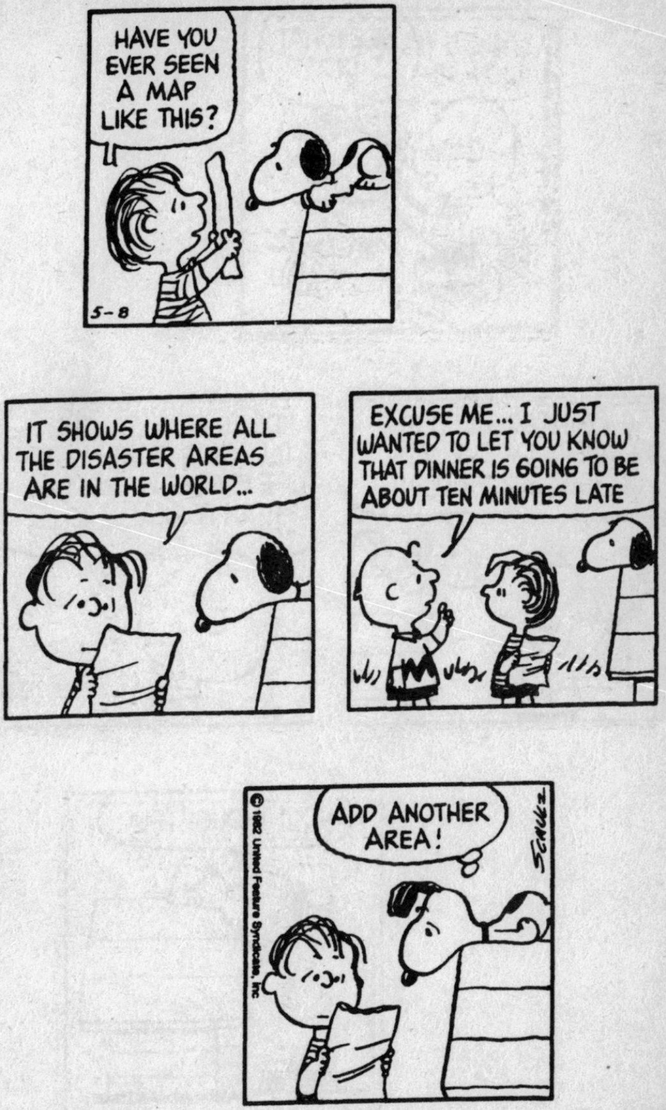
HAVE YOU EVER SEEN A MAP LIKE THIS?
5-8
IT SHOWS WHERE ALL THE DISASTER AREAS ARE IN THE WORLD...
EXCUSE ME... I JUST WANTED TO LET YOU KNOW THAT DINNER IS GOING TO BE ABOUT TEN MINUTES LATE
ADD ANOTHER AREA!
© 1982 United Feature Syndicate, Inc
SCHULZ

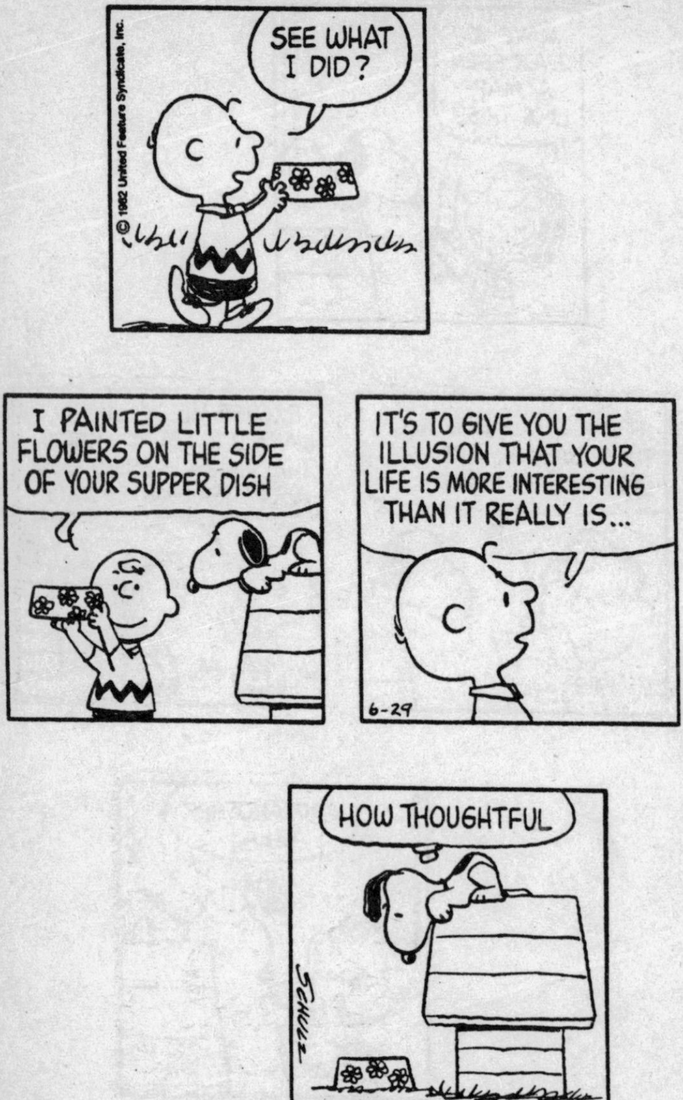
SEE WHAT I DID?
© 1982 United Feature Syndicate, Inc.
I PAINTED LITTLE FLOWERS ON THE SIDE OF YOUR SUPPER DISH
IT'S TO GIVE YOU THE ILLUSION THAT YOUR LIFE IS MORE INTERESTING THAN IT REALLY IS...
6-29
HOW THOUGHTFUL
SCHULZ

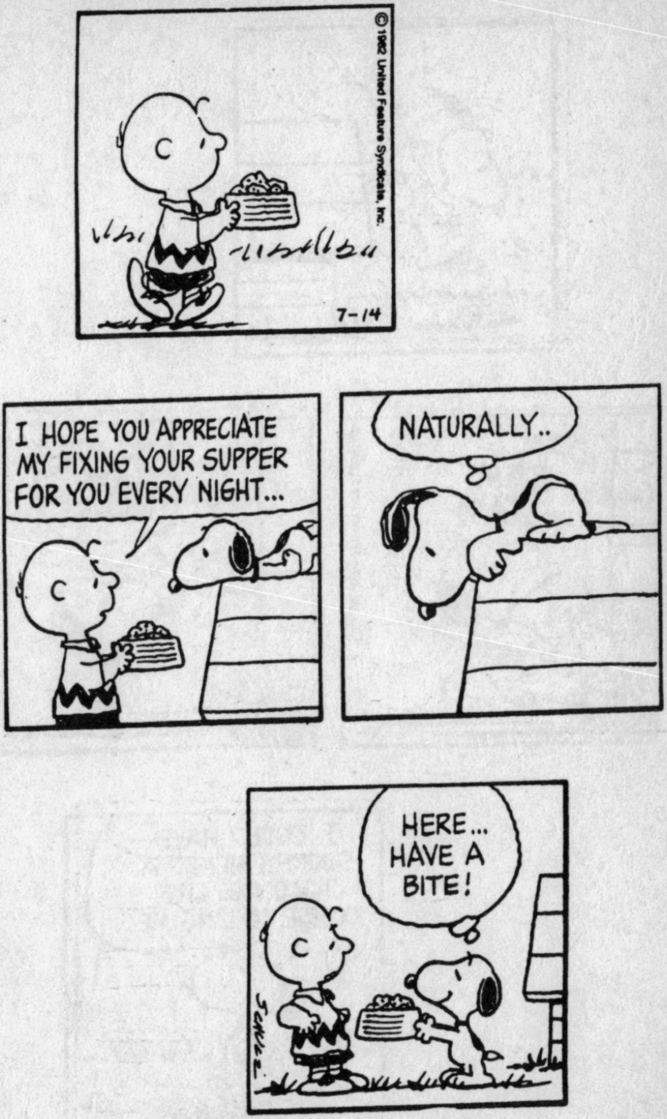
© 1982 United Feature Syndicate, Inc.
7-14
I HOPE YOU APPRECIATE MY FIXING YOUR SUPPER FOR YOU EVERY NIGHT...
NATURALLY..
HERE... HAVE A BITE!

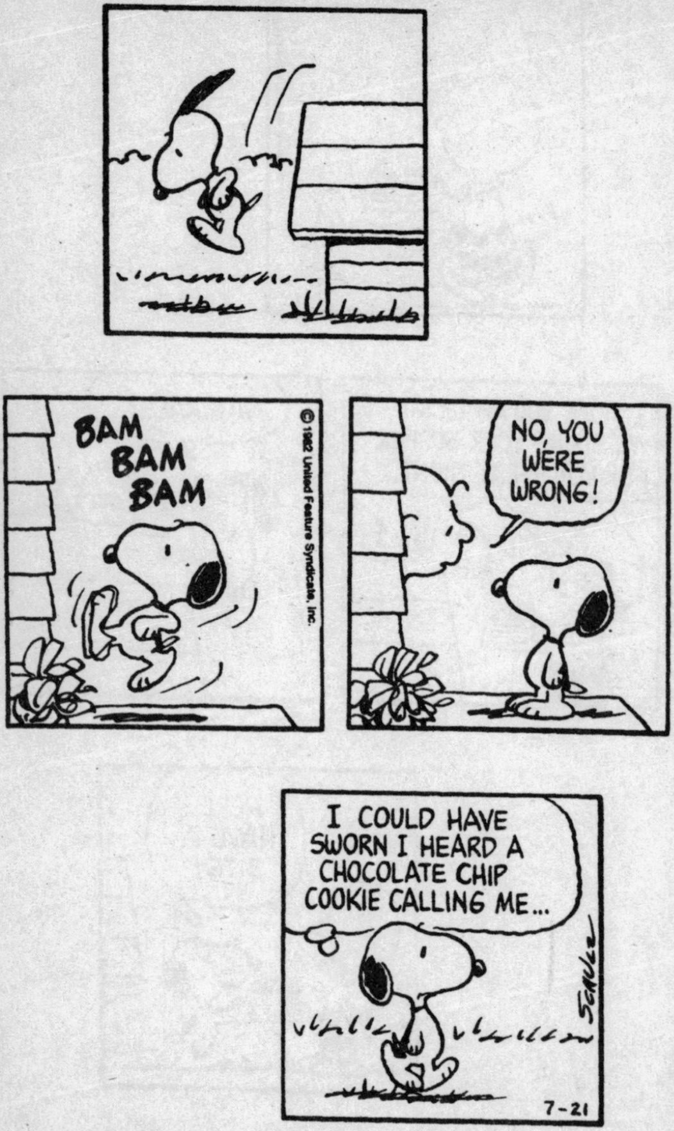
BAM
BAM
BAM
© 1982 United Feature Syndicate, Inc.
NO, YOU WERE WRONG!
I COULD HAVE SWORN I HEARD A CHOCOLATE CHIP COOKIE CALLING ME...
SCHULZ
7-21

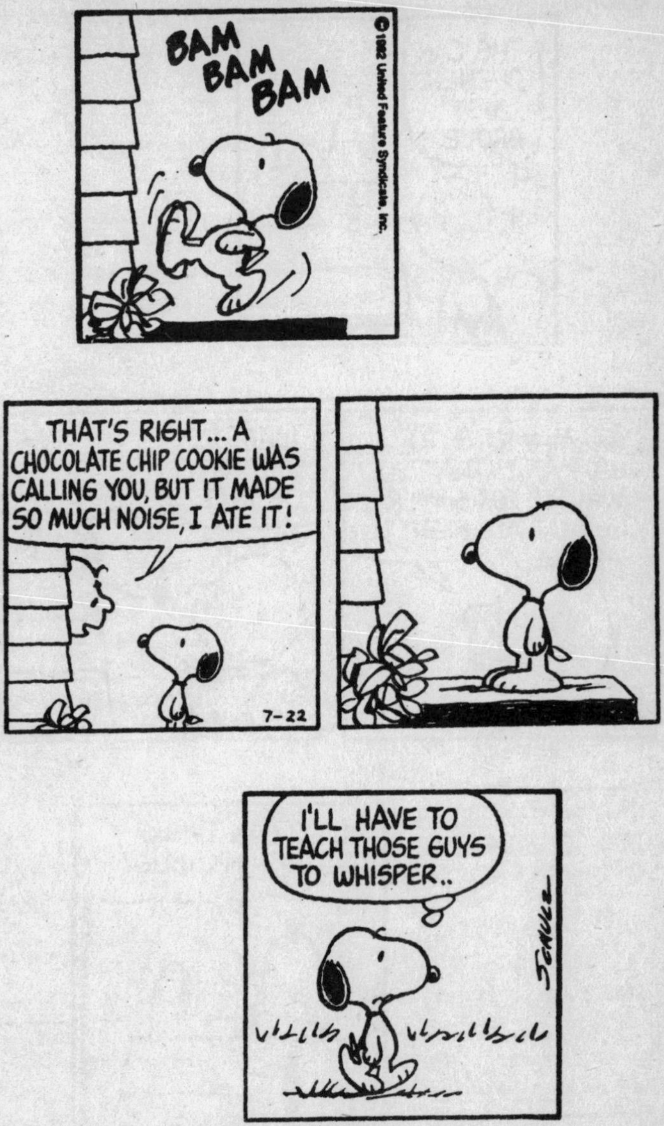
BAM
BAM
BAM
© 1982 United Feature Syndicate, Inc.
THAT'S RIGHT... A CHOCOLATE CHIP COOKIE WAS CALLING YOU, BUT IT MADE SO MUCH NOISE, I ATE IT!
7-22
I'LL HAVE TO TEACH THOSE GUYS TO WHISPER..
SCHULZ

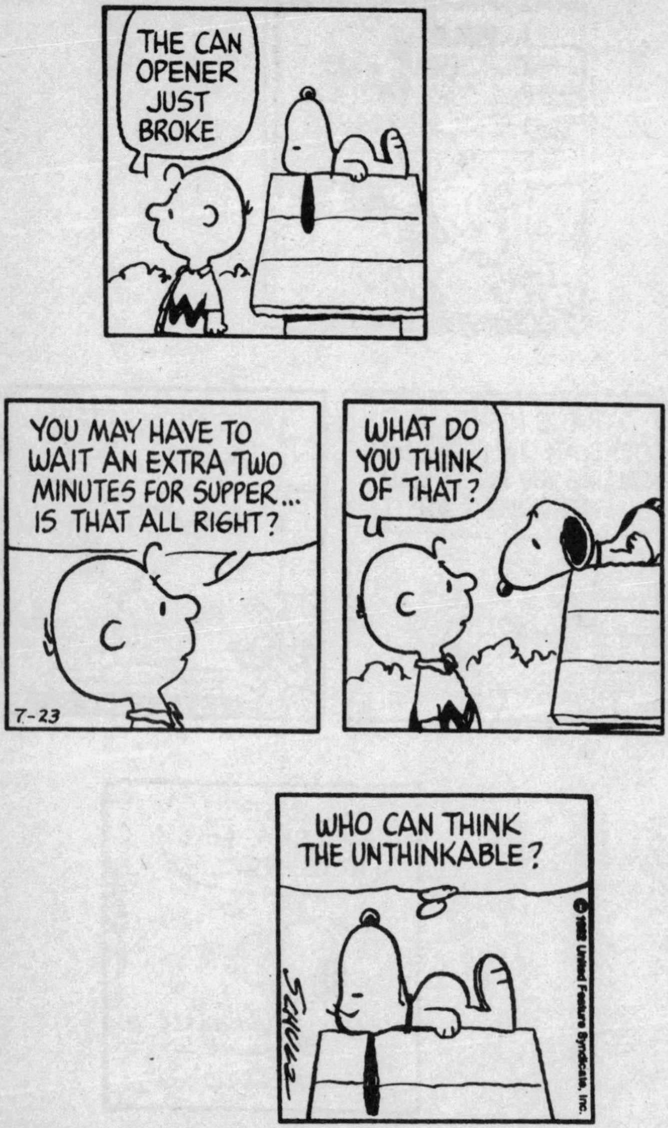
THE CAN OPENER JUST BROKE
YOU MAY HAVE TO WAIT AN EXTRA TWO MINUTES FOR SUPPER... IS THAT ALL RIGHT?
7-23
WHAT DO YOU THINK OF THAT?
WHO CAN THINK THE UNTHINKABLE?
SCHULZ

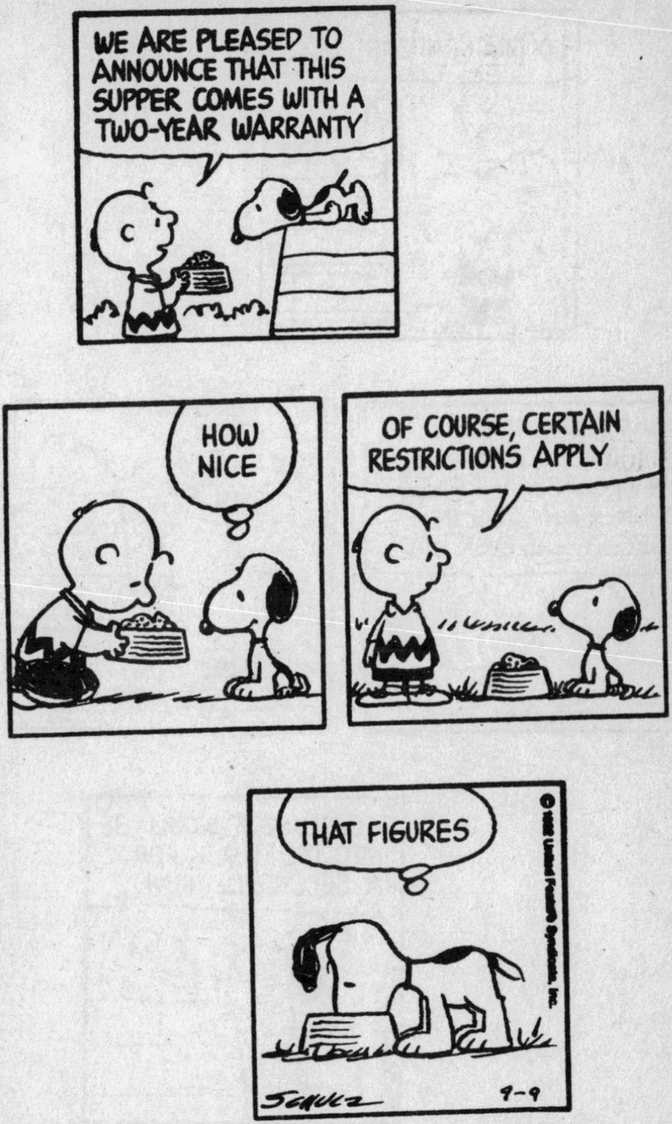
WE ARE PLEASED TO ANNOUNCE THAT THIS SUPPER COMES WITH A TWO-YEAR WARRANTY
HOW NICE
OF COURSE, CERTAIN RESTRICTIONS APPLY
THAT FIGURES
SCHULZ
9-9

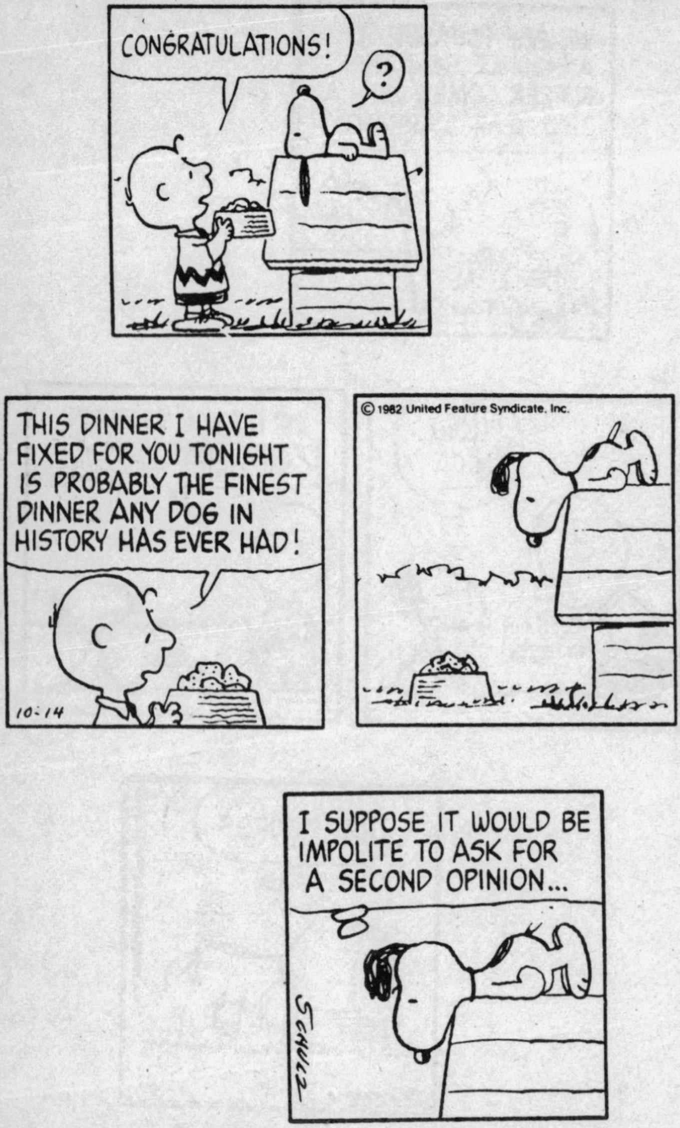
CONGRATULATIONS!
?
THIS DINNER I HAVE FIXED FOR YOU TONIGHT IS PROBABLY THE FINEST DINNER ANY DOG IN HISTORY HAS EVER HAD!
10-14
© 1982 United Feature Syndicate, Inc.
I SUPPOSE IT WOULD BE IMPOLITE TO ASK FOR A SECOND OPINION...
SCHULZ

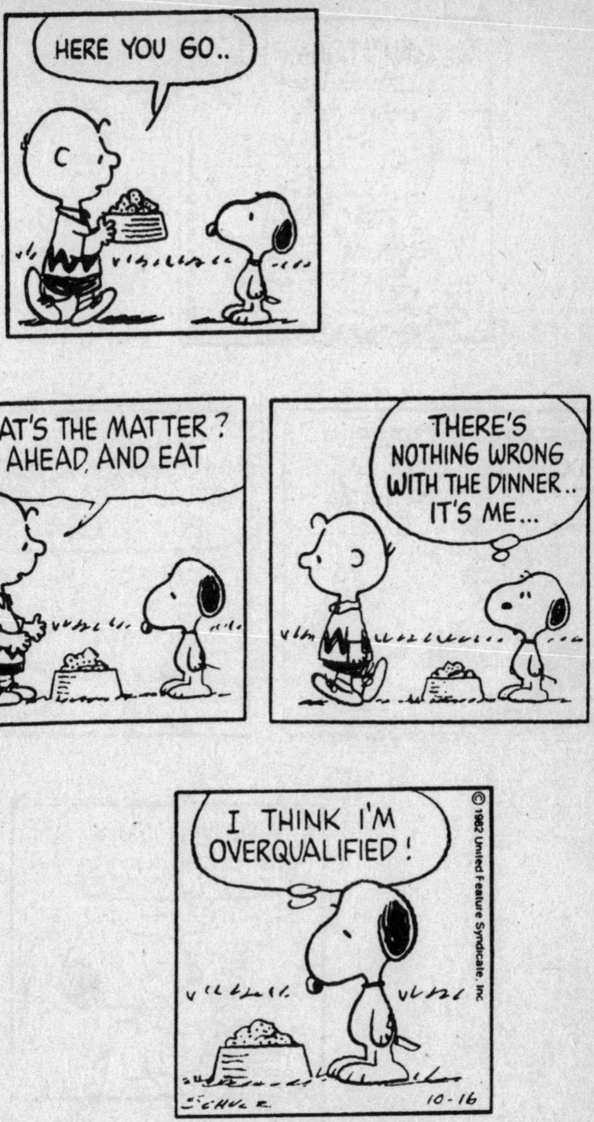
HERE YOU GO..
WHAT'S THE MATTER ? GO AHEAD, AND EAT
THERE'S NOTHING WRONG WITH THE DINNER.. IT'S ME...
I THINK I'M OVERQUALIFIED !
© 1982 United Feature Syndicate, Inc
10-16

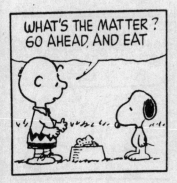

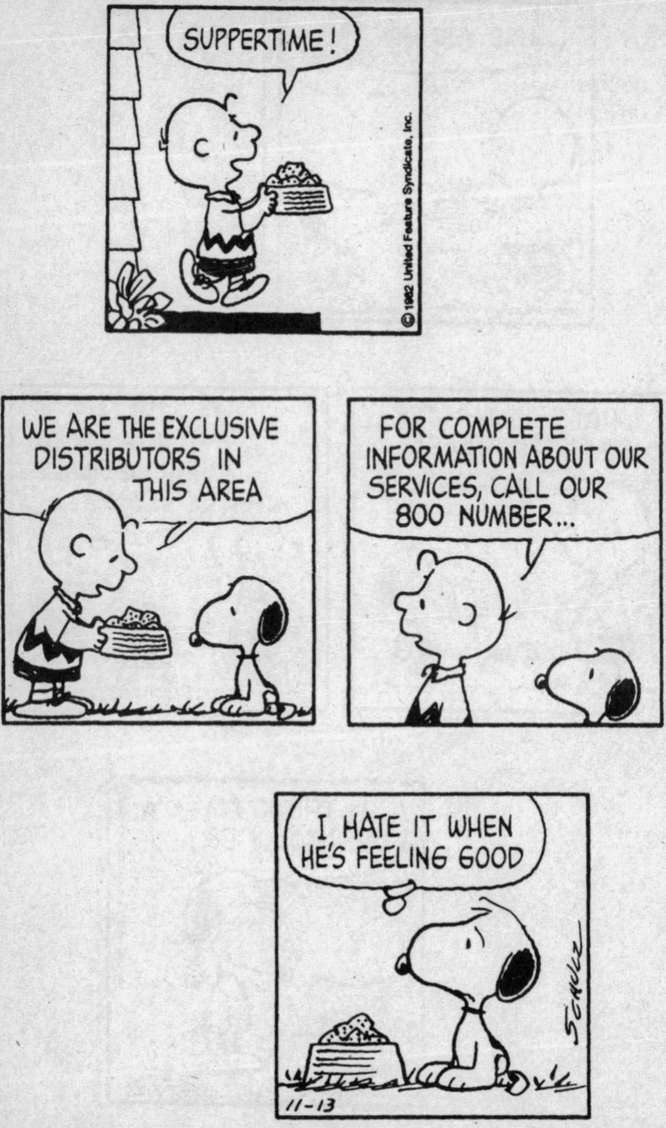
SUPPERTIME!
© 1982 United Feature Syndicate, Inc.
WE ARE THE EXCLUSIVE DISTRIBUTORS IN THIS AREA
FOR COMPLETE INFORMATION ABOUT OUR SERVICES, CALL OUR 800 NUMBER...
I HATE IT WHEN HE'S FEELING GOOD
SCHULZ
11-13

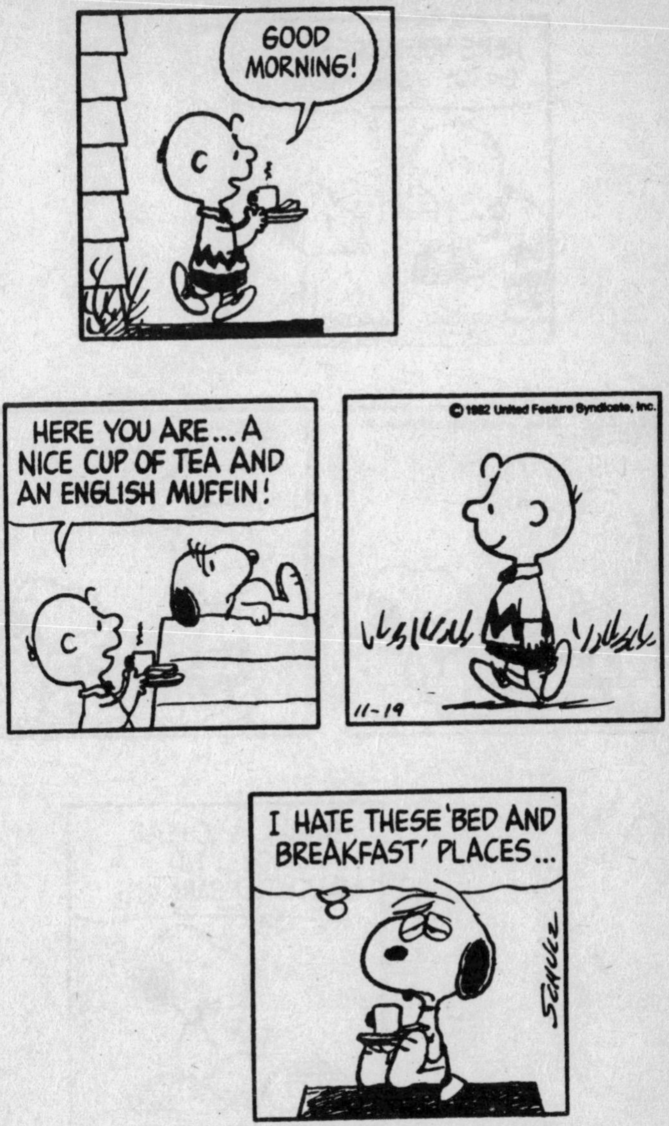
GOOD MORNING!
HERE YOU ARE... A NICE CUP OF TEA AND AN ENGLISH MUFFIN!
© 1982 United Feature Syndicate, Inc.
11-19
I HATE THESE 'BED AND BREAKFAST' PLACES...

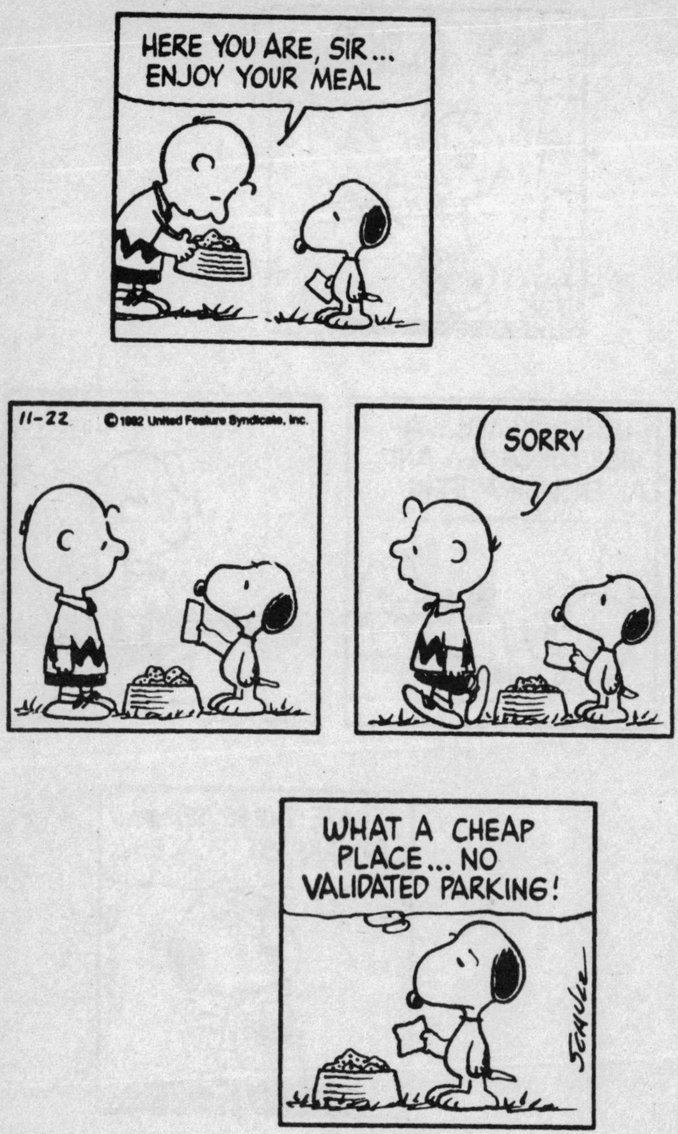
HERE YOU ARE, SIR...
ENJOY YOUR MEAL
11-22
© 1982 United Feature Syndicate, Inc.
SORRY
WHAT A CHEAP PLACE... NO VALIDATED PARKING!
SCHULZ

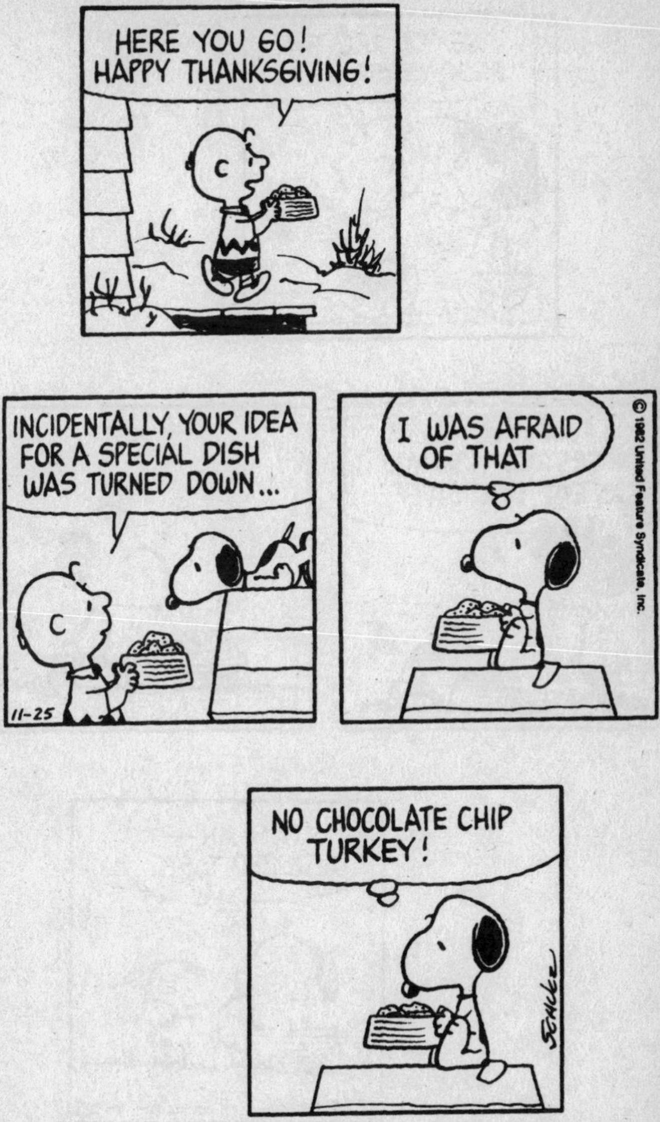
HERE YOU GO! HAPPY THANKSGIVING!
INCIDENTALLY, YOUR IDEA FOR A SPECIAL DISH WAS TURNED DOWN...
11-25
I WAS AFRAID OF THAT
© 1982 United Feature Syndicate, Inc.
NO CHOCOLATE CHIP TURKEY!
SCHULZ

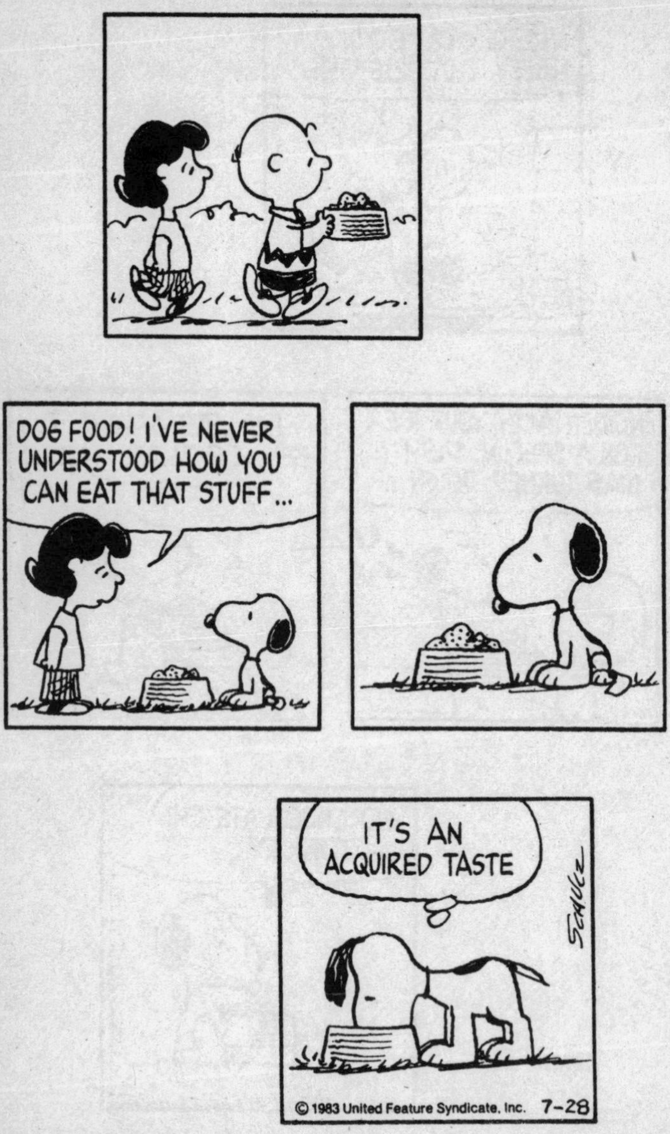
DOG FOOD! I'VE NEVER UNDERSTOOD HOW YOU CAN EAT THAT STUFF...
IT'S AN ACQUIRED TASTE
SCHULZ
© 1983 United Feature Syndicate, Inc. 7-28

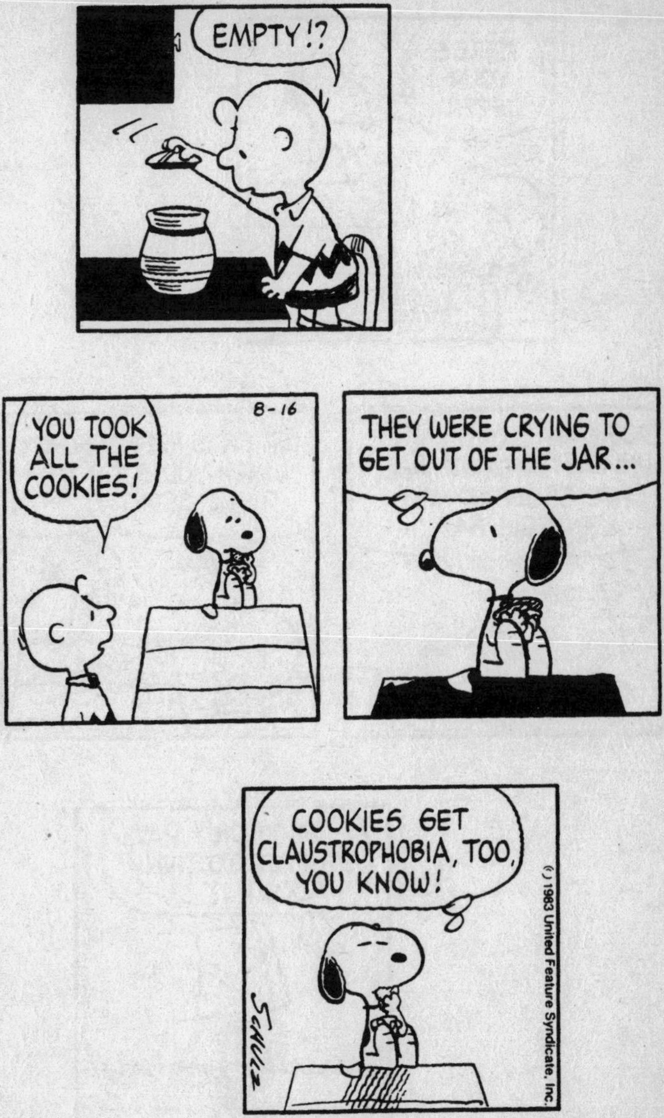
EMPTY!?
8-16
YOU TOOK ALL THE COOKIES!
THEY WERE CRYING TO GET OUT OF THE JAR...
COOKIES GET CLAUSTROPHOBIA, TOO, YOU KNOW!
SCHULZ
© 1983 United Feature Syndicate, Inc.

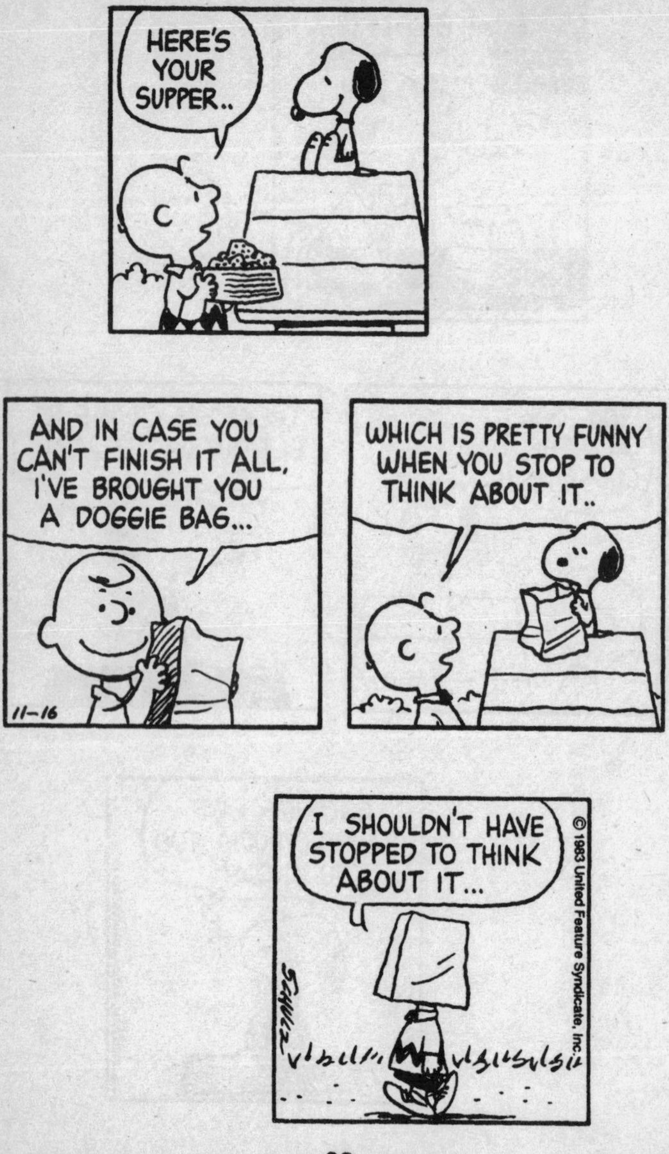
HERE'S YOUR SUPPER..
AND IN CASE YOU CAN'T FINISH IT ALL, I'VE BROUGHT YOU A DOGGIE BAG...
11-16
WHICH IS PRETTY FUNNY WHEN YOU STOP TO THINK ABOUT IT..
I SHOULDN'T HAVE STOPPED TO THINK ABOUT IT...
SCHULZ
© 1983 United Feature Syndicate, Inc.

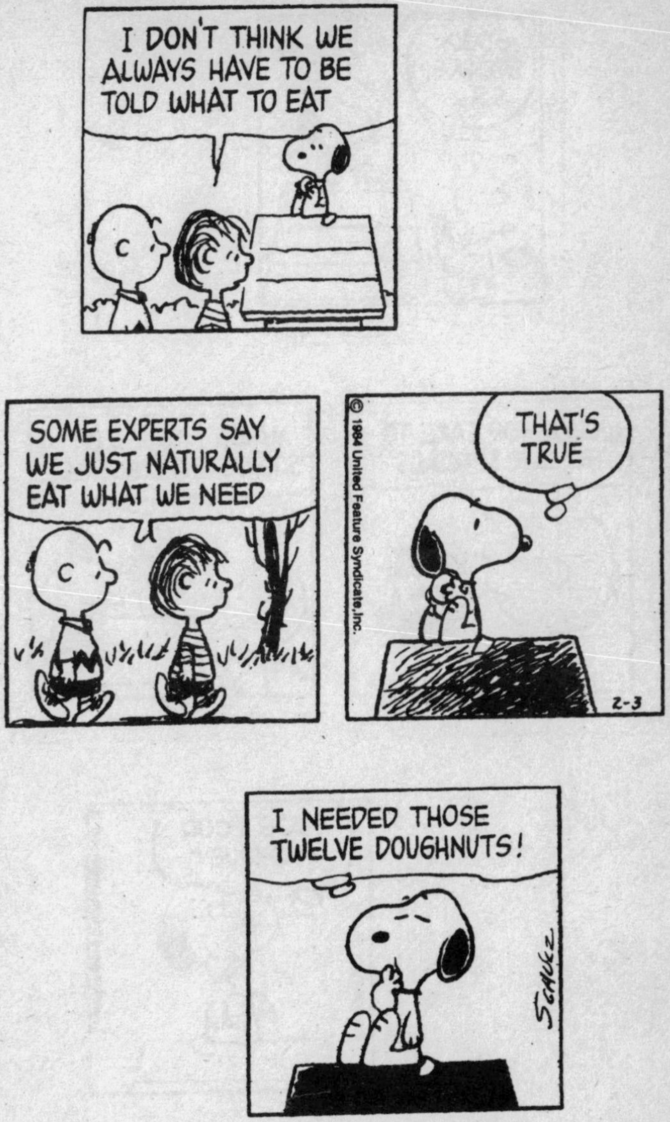
I DON'T THINK WE ALWAYS HAVE TO BE TOLD WHAT TO EAT
SOME EXPERTS SAY WE JUST NATURALLY EAT WHAT WE NEED
© 1984 United Feature Syndicate, Inc.
THAT'S TRUE
2-3
I NEEDED THOSE TWELVE DOUGHNUTS!

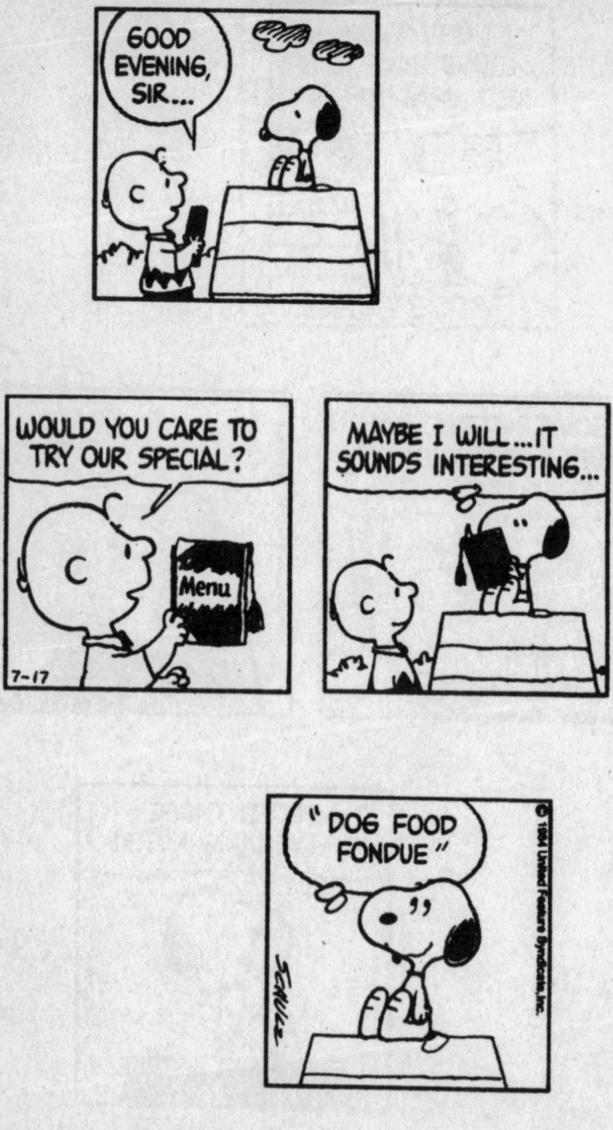
GOOD EVENING, SIR...
WOULD YOU CARE TO TRY OUR SPECIAL?
Menu
7-17
MAYBE I WILL...IT SOUNDS INTERESTING...
"DOG FOOD FONDUE"
SCHULZ
© 1984 United Feature Syndicate, Inc.

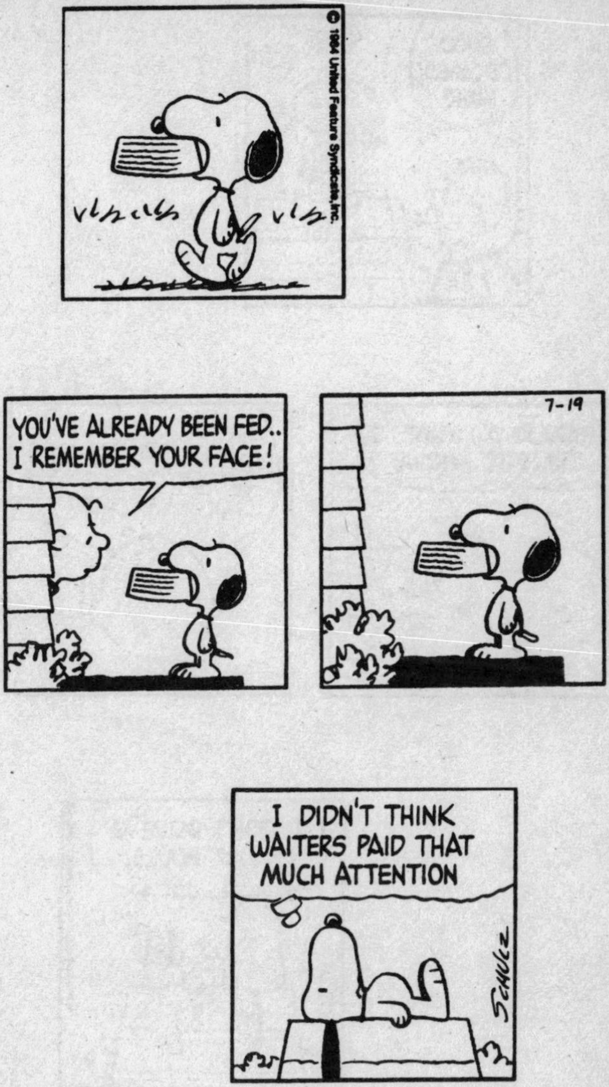
© 1984 United Feature Syndicate, Inc.
YOU'VE ALREADY BEEN FED.. I REMEMBER YOUR FACE!
7-19
I DIDN'T THINK WAITERS PAID THAT MUCH ATTENTION
SCHULZ

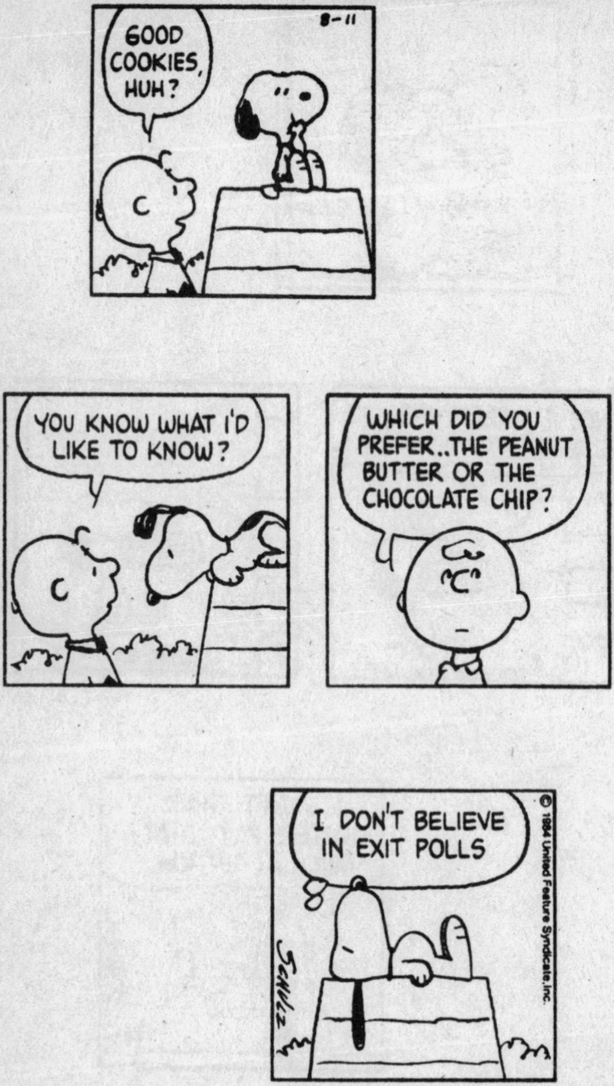
8-11
GOOD COOKIES, HUH?
YOU KNOW WHAT I'D LIKE TO KNOW?
WHICH DID YOU PREFER..THE PEANUT BUTTER OR THE CHOCOLATE CHIP?
I DON'T BELIEVE IN EXIT POLLS
© 1984 United Feature Syndicate, Inc.

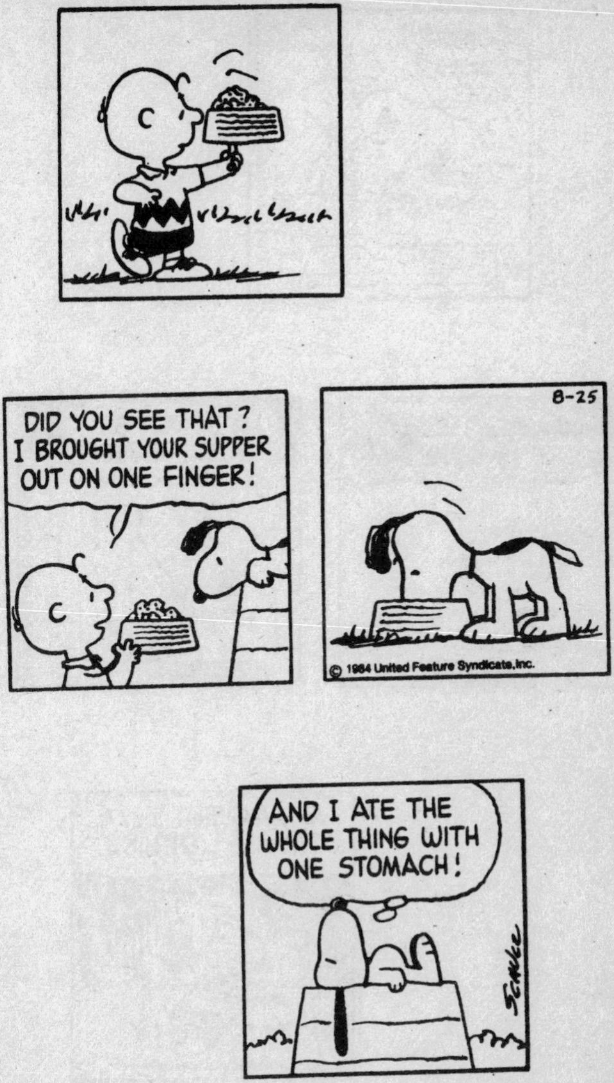
DID YOU SEE THAT ? I BROUGHT YOUR SUPPER OUT ON ONE FINGER !
8-25
AND I ATE THE WHOLE THING WITH ONE STOMACH !

OH OH!
I'D BETTER GO IN THE HOUSE..
I'VE HEARD THAT PIZZA ATTRACTS LIGHTNING!
SCHULZ
9-24

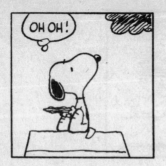

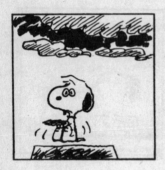

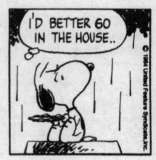

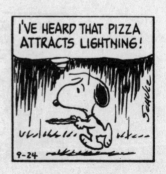

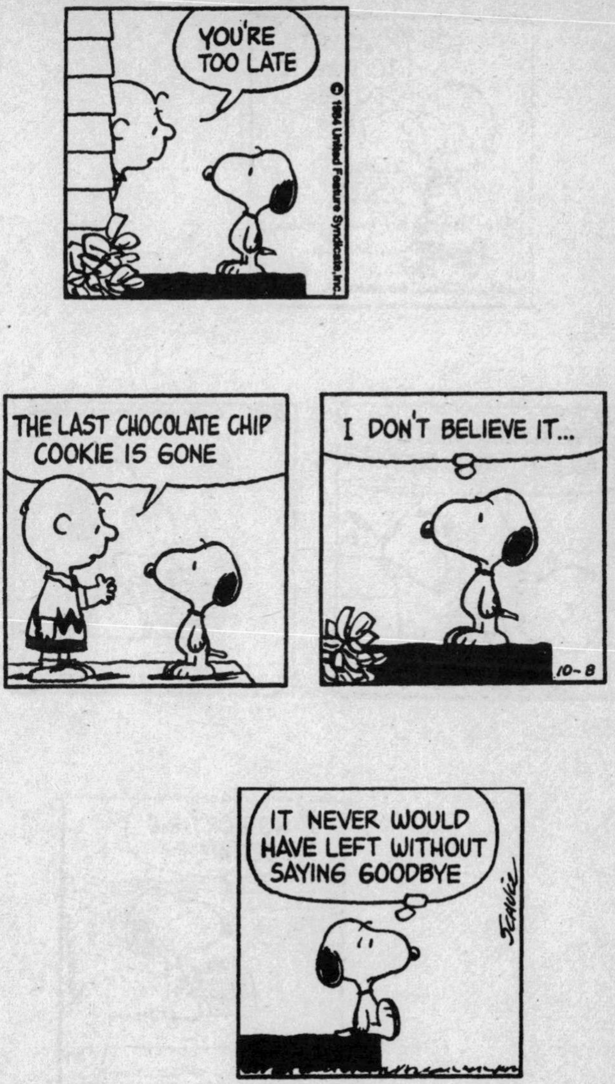
YOU'RE TOO LATE
© 1984 United Feature Syndicate, Inc.
THE LAST CHOCOLATE CHIP COOKIE IS GONE
I DON'T BELIEVE IT...
10-8
IT NEVER WOULD HAVE LEFT WITHOUT SAYING GOODBYE
SCHULZ

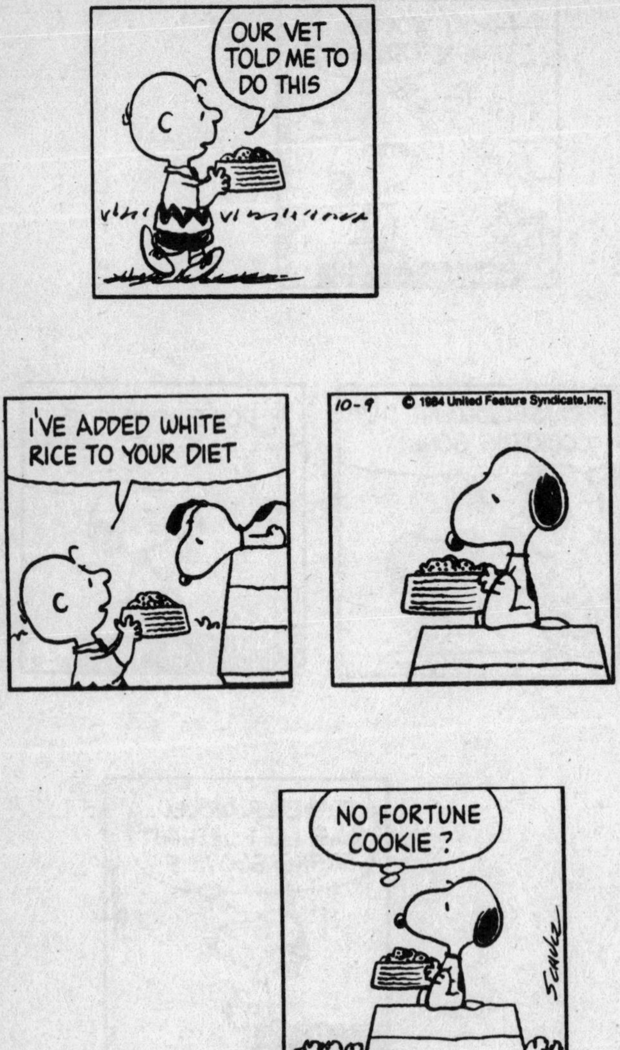
OUR VET TOLD ME TO DO THIS
I'VE ADDED WHITE RICE TO YOUR DIET
10-9
© 1984 United Feature Syndicate, Inc.
NO FORTUNE COOKIE ?
SCHULZ

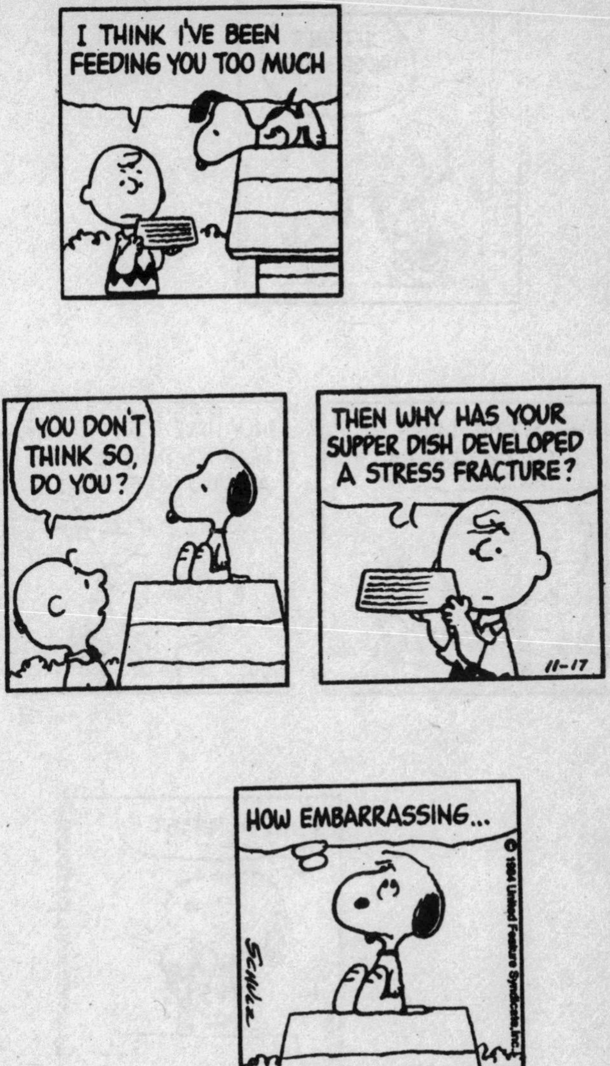

I THINK I'VE BEEN FEEDING YOU TOO MUCH
YOU DON'T THINK SO, DO YOU?
THEN WHY HAS YOUR SUPPER DISH DEVELOPED A STRESS FRACTURE?
11-17
HOW EMBARRASSING...
SCHULZ
© 1984 United Feature Syndicate, Inc.

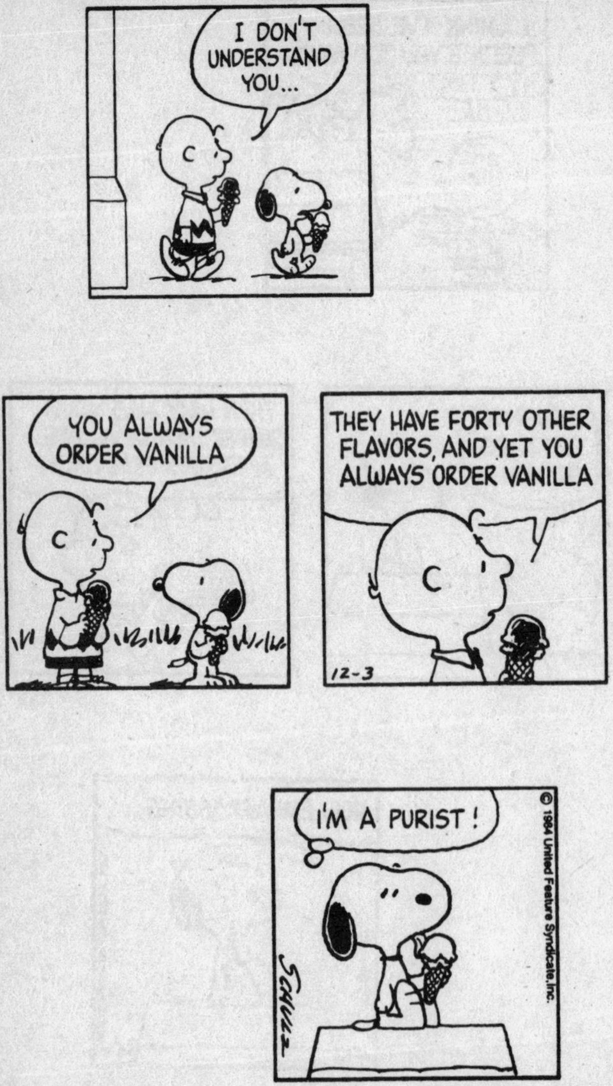
I DON'T UNDERSTAND YOU...
YOU ALWAYS ORDER VANILLA
THEY HAVE FORTY OTHER FLAVORS, AND YET YOU ALWAYS ORDER VANILLA
12-3
I'M A PURIST!
SCHULZ
© 1984 United Feature Syndicate, Inc.

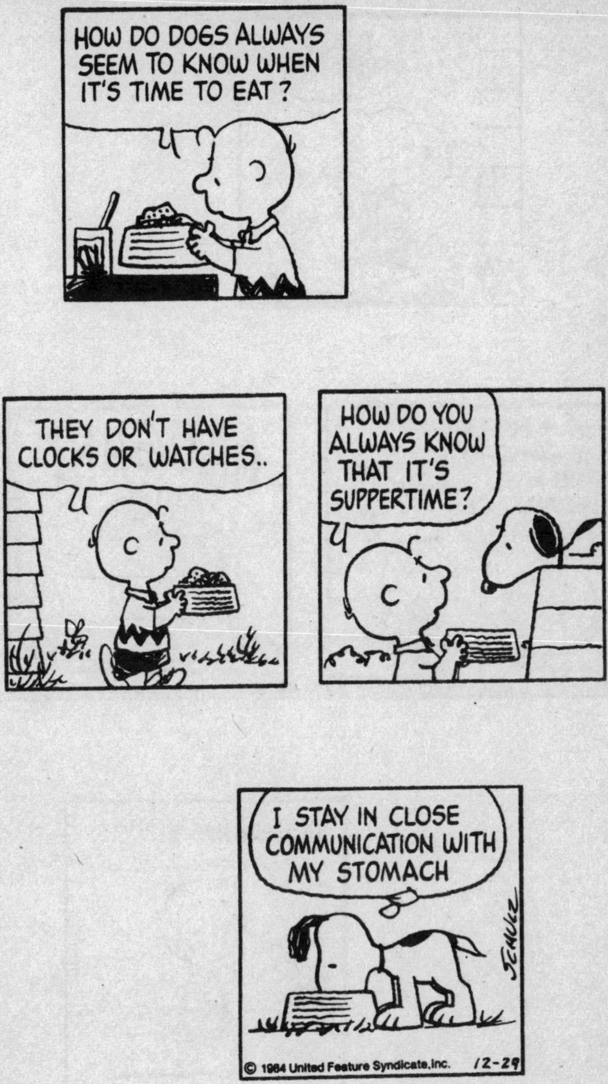
HOW DO DOGS ALWAYS SEEM TO KNOW WHEN IT'S TIME TO EAT?
THEY DON'T HAVE CLOCKS OR WATCHES..
HOW DO YOU ALWAYS KNOW THAT IT'S SUPPERTIME?
I STAY IN CLOSE COMMUNICATION WITH MY STOMACH
SCHULZ
© 1984 United Feature Syndicate, Inc. 12-29

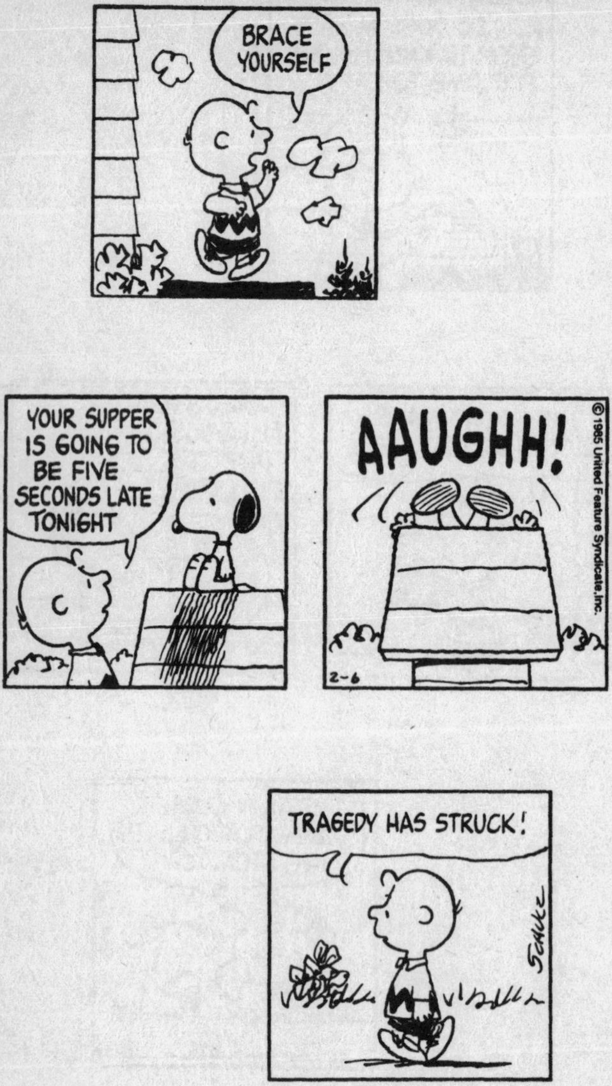
BRACE YOURSELF
YOUR SUPPER IS GOING TO BE FIVE SECONDS LATE TONIGHT
AAUGHH!
© 1985 United Feature Syndicate, Inc.
2-6
TRAGEDY HAS STRUCK!
SCHULZ

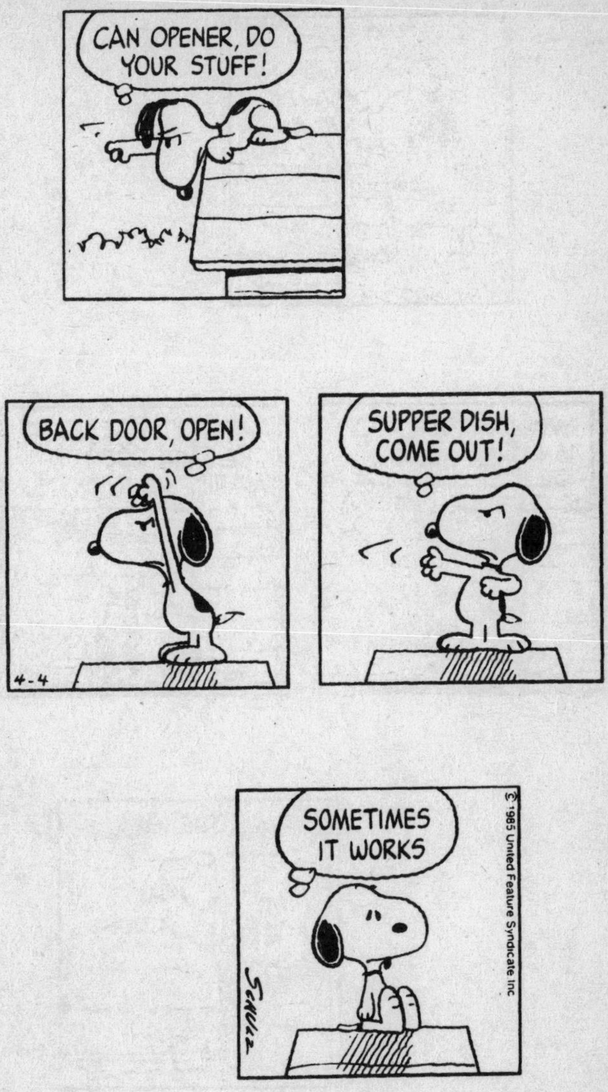
CAN OPENER, DO YOUR STUFF!
BACK DOOR, OPEN!
4-4
SUPPER DISH, COME OUT!
SOMETIMES IT WORKS
© 1985 United Feature Syndicate Inc

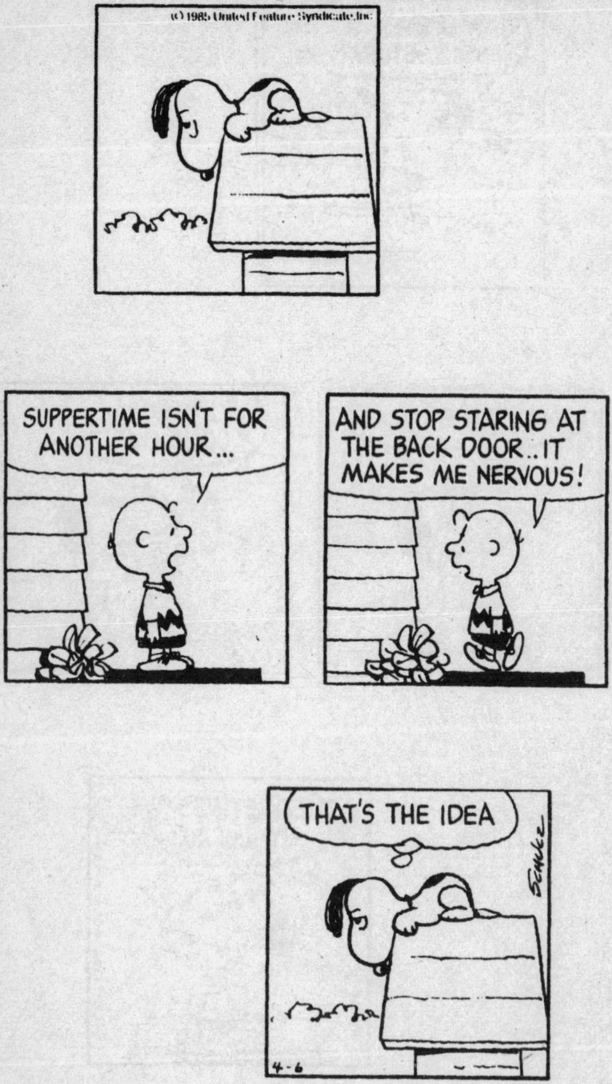
© 1985 United Feature Syndicate, Inc
SUPPERTIME ISN'T FOR ANOTHER HOUR...
AND STOP STARING AT THE BACK DOOR.. IT MAKES ME NERVOUS!
THAT'S THE IDEA
SCHULZ
4-6

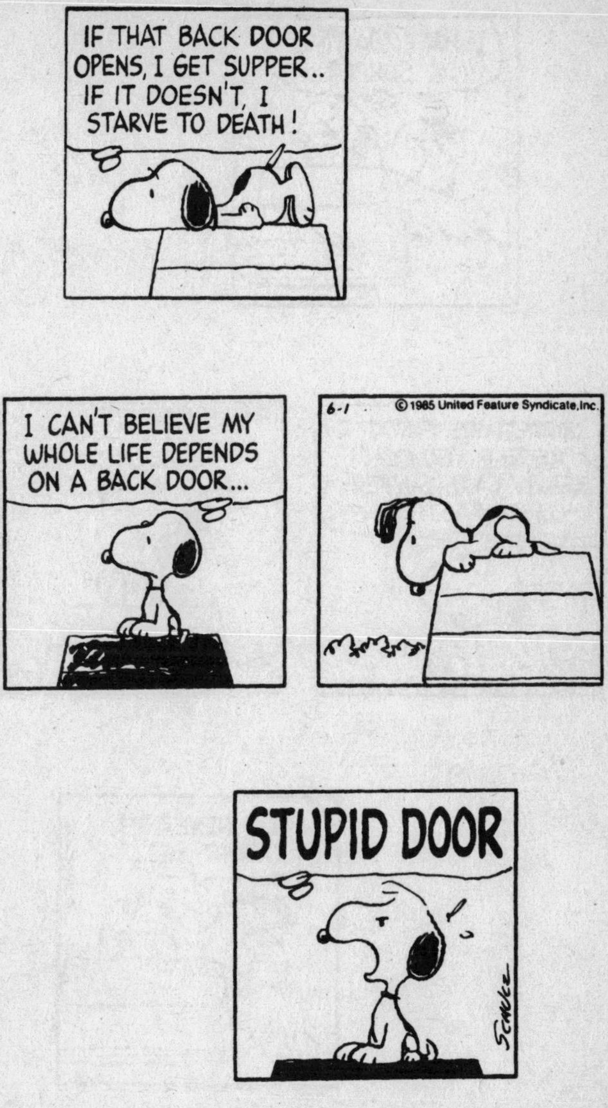
IF THAT BACK DOOR OPENS, I GET SUPPER.. IF IT DOESN'T, I STARVE TO DEATH!
I CAN'T BELIEVE MY WHOLE LIFE DEPENDS ON A BACK DOOR...
6-1
© 1985 United Feature Syndicate, Inc.
STUPID DOOR

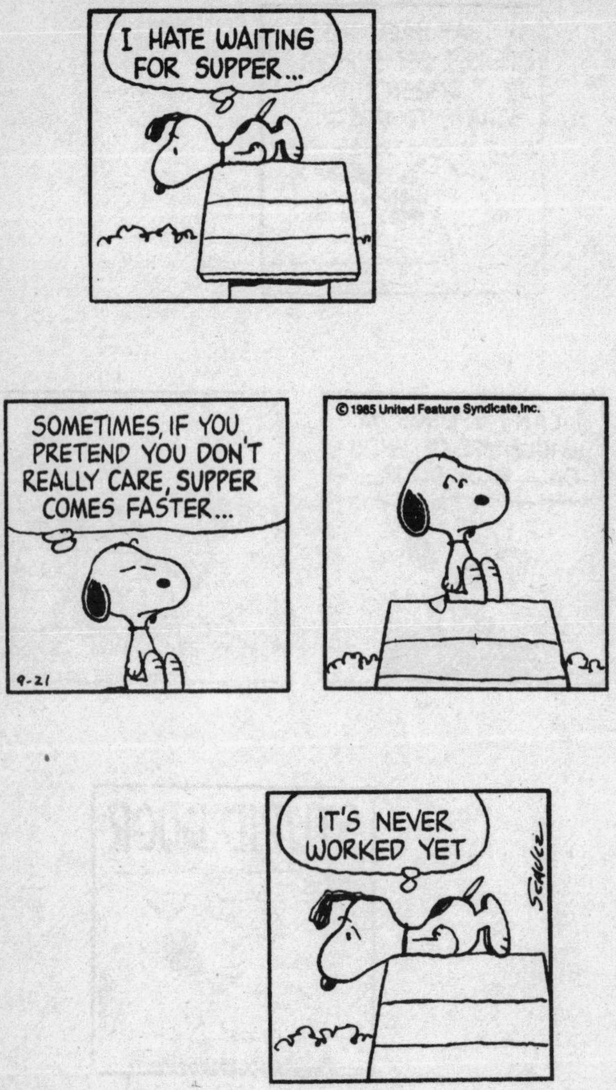
I HATE WAITING FOR SUPPER...
SOMETIMES, IF YOU PRETEND YOU DON'T REALLY CARE, SUPPER COMES FASTER...
9-21
© 1985 United Feature Syndicate, Inc.
IT'S NEVER WORKED YET
SCHULZ

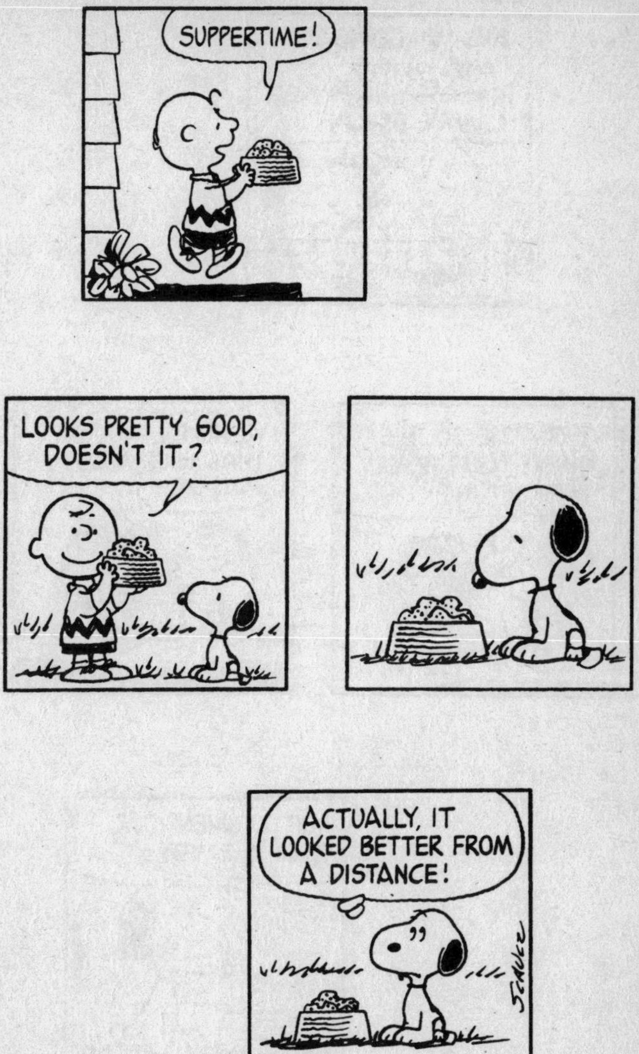
SUPPERTIME!
LOOKS PRETTY GOOD, DOESN'T IT?
ACTUALLY, IT LOOKED BETTER FROM A DISTANCE!
SCHULZ
© 1985 United Feature Syndicate, Inc.
9-12

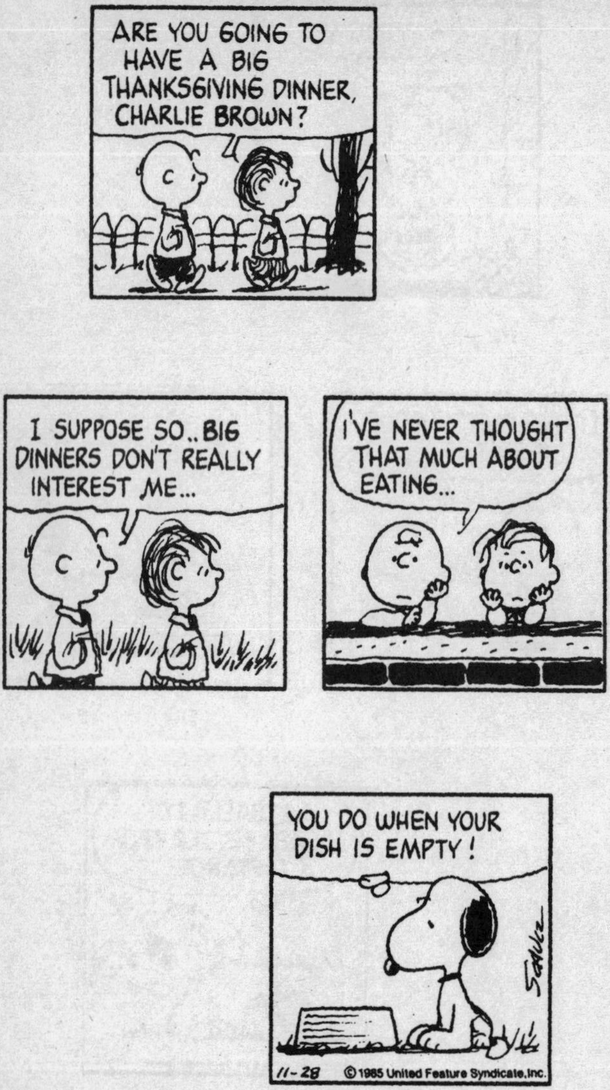
ARE YOU GOING TO HAVE A BIG THANKSGIVING DINNER, CHARLIE BROWN?
I SUPPOSE SO.. BIG DINNERS DON'T REALLY INTEREST ME...
I'VE NEVER THOUGHT THAT MUCH ABOUT EATING...
YOU DO WHEN YOUR DISH IS EMPTY!
SCHULZ
11-28
©1985 United Feature Syndicate, Inc.

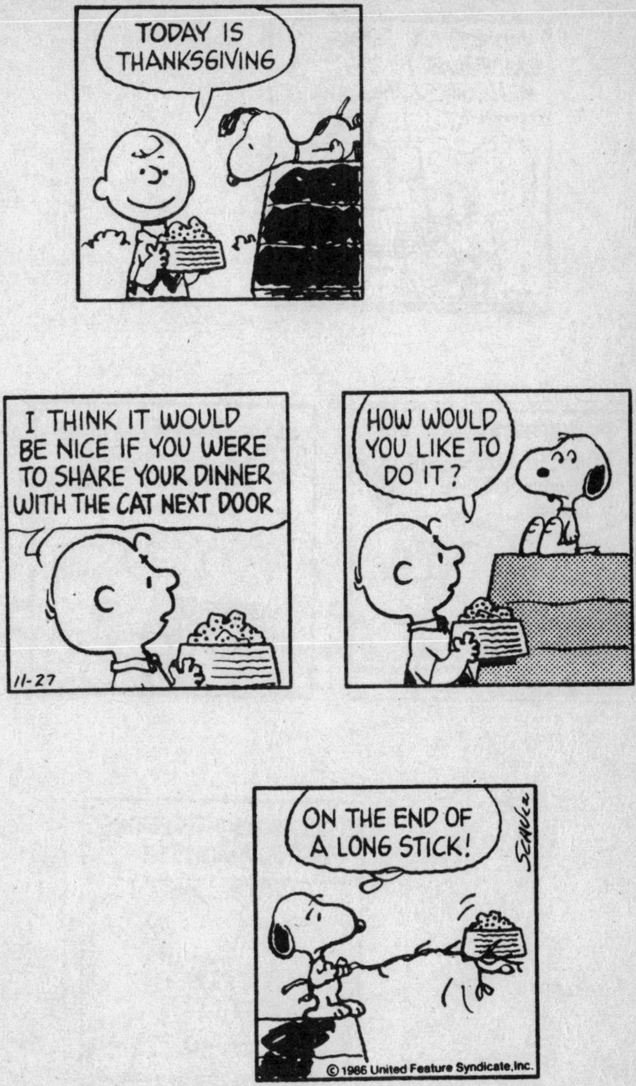
TODAY IS THANKSGIVING
I THINK IT WOULD BE NICE IF YOU WERE TO SHARE YOUR DINNER WITH THE CAT NEXT DOOR
11-27
HOW WOULD YOU LIKE TO DO IT?
ON THE END OF A LONG STICK!
SCHULZ
© 1986 United Feature Syndicate, Inc.

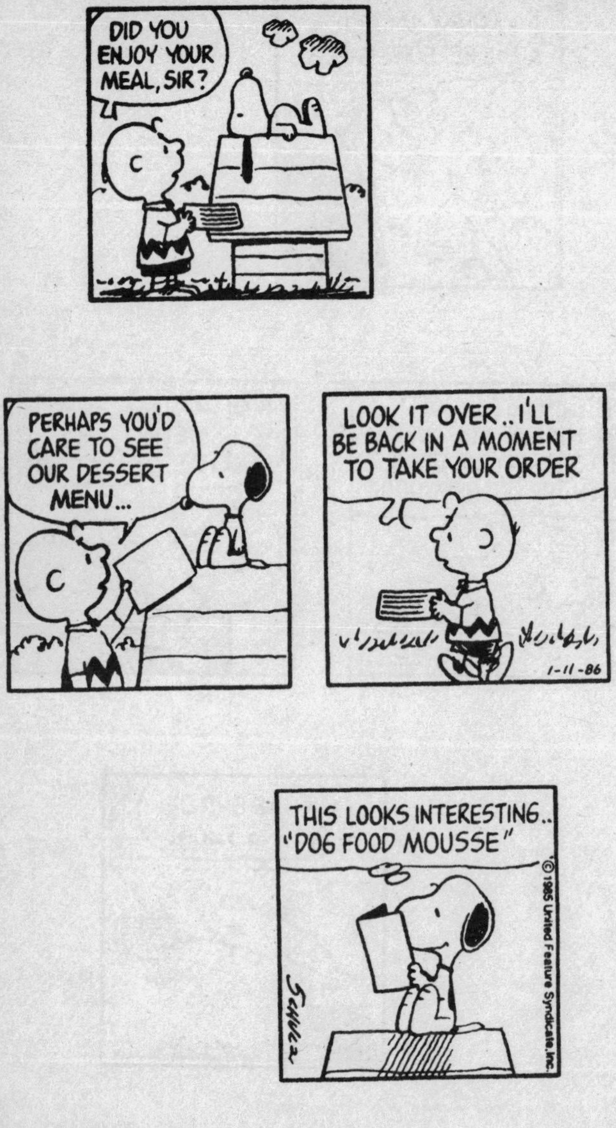
DID YOU ENJOY YOUR MEAL, SIR?
PERHAPS YOU'D CARE TO SEE OUR DESSERT MENU...
LOOK IT OVER..I'LL BE BACK IN A MOMENT TO TAKE YOUR ORDER
1-11-86
THIS LOOKS INTERESTING..
"DOG FOOD MOUSSE"
SCHULZ
© 1985 United Feature Syndicate, Inc.

I KNOW I SAW THEIR AD HERE SOMEPLACE..
"PIZZA TO GO"... "PIZZA TO ORDER"..
"PIZZA AT YOUR DOOR"...
© 1986 United Feature Syndicate, Inc.
1-29
AH, HERE IT IS... "PIZZA FOR RENT"
SCHULZ

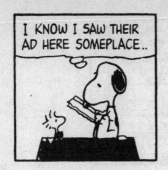

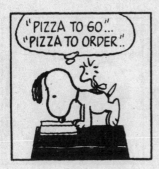

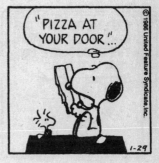

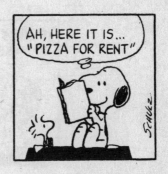

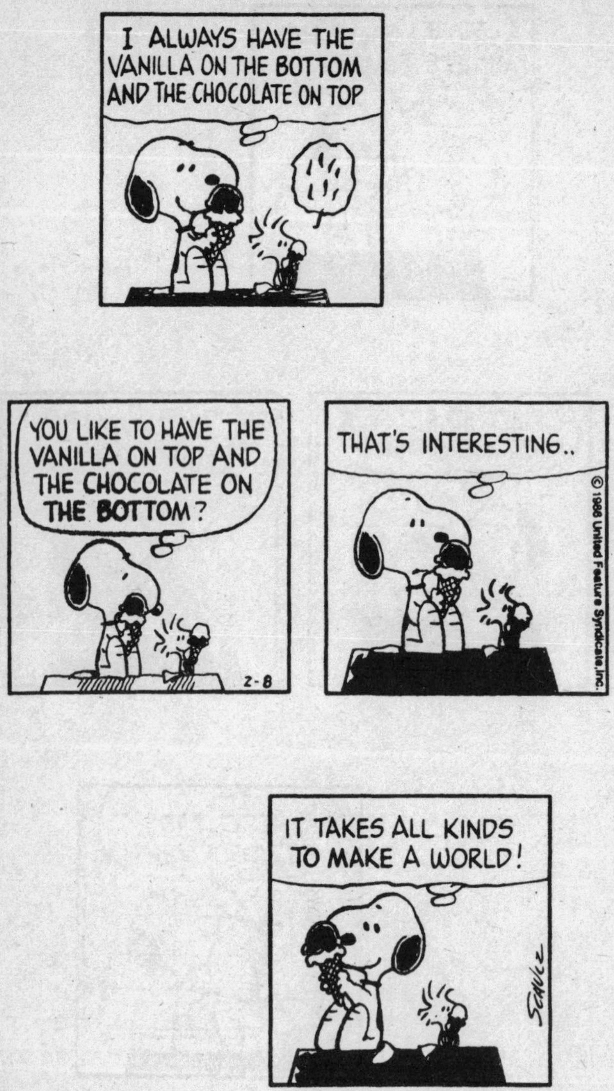
I ALWAYS HAVE THE VANILLA ON THE BOTTOM AND THE CHOCOLATE ON TOP
YOU LIKE TO HAVE THE VANILLA ON TOP AND THE CHOCOLATE ON THE BOTTOM?
2-8
THAT'S INTERESTING..
© 1988 United Feature Syndicate, Inc.
IT TAKES ALL KINDS TO MAKE A WORLD!
SCHULZ

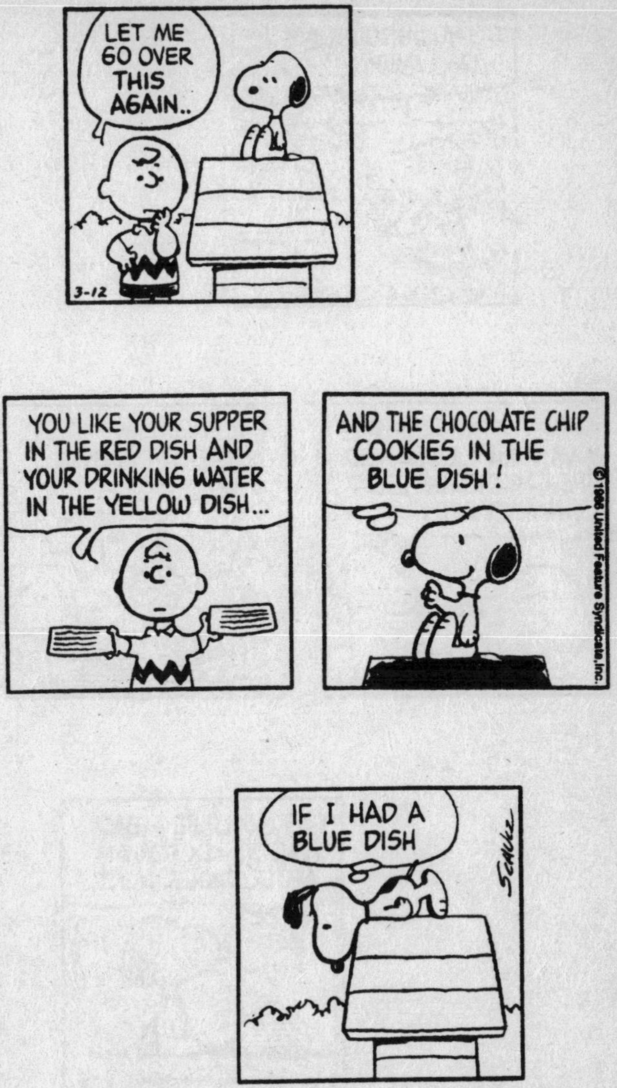
LET ME GO OVER THIS AGAIN..
3-12
YOU LIKE YOUR SUPPER IN THE RED DISH AND YOUR DRINKING WATER IN THE YELLOW DISH...
AND THE CHOCOLATE CHIP COOKIES IN THE BLUE DISH!
© 1988 United Feature Syndicate, Inc.
IF I HAD A BLUE DISH
SCHULZ

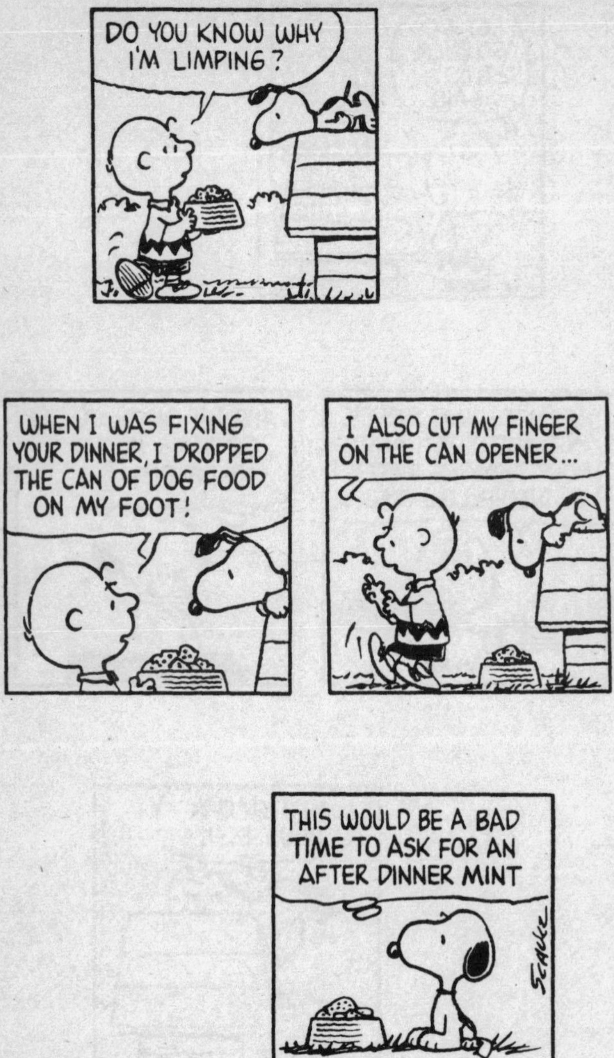
DO YOU KNOW WHY I'M LIMPING?
WHEN I WAS FIXING YOUR DINNER, I DROPPED THE CAN OF DOG FOOD ON MY FOOT!
I ALSO CUT MY FINGER ON THE CAN OPENER...
THIS WOULD BE A BAD TIME TO ASK FOR AN AFTER DINNER MINT
SCHULZ
© 1986 United Feature Syndicate, Inc.
4-8

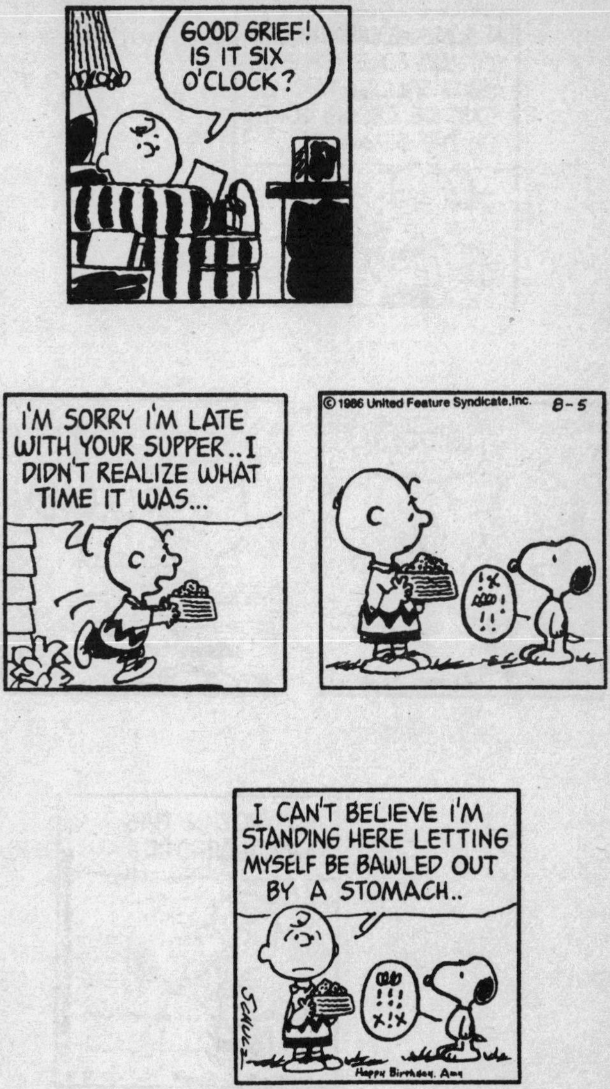
GOOD GRIEF! IS IT SIX O'CLOCK?
I'M SORRY I'M LATE WITH YOUR SUPPER..I DIDN'T REALIZE WHAT TIME IT WAS...
© 1986 United Feature Syndicate,Inc.
8-5
I CAN'T BELIEVE I'M STANDING HERE LETTING MYSELF BE BAWLED OUT BY A STOMACH..
SCHULZ
Happy Birthday, Amy

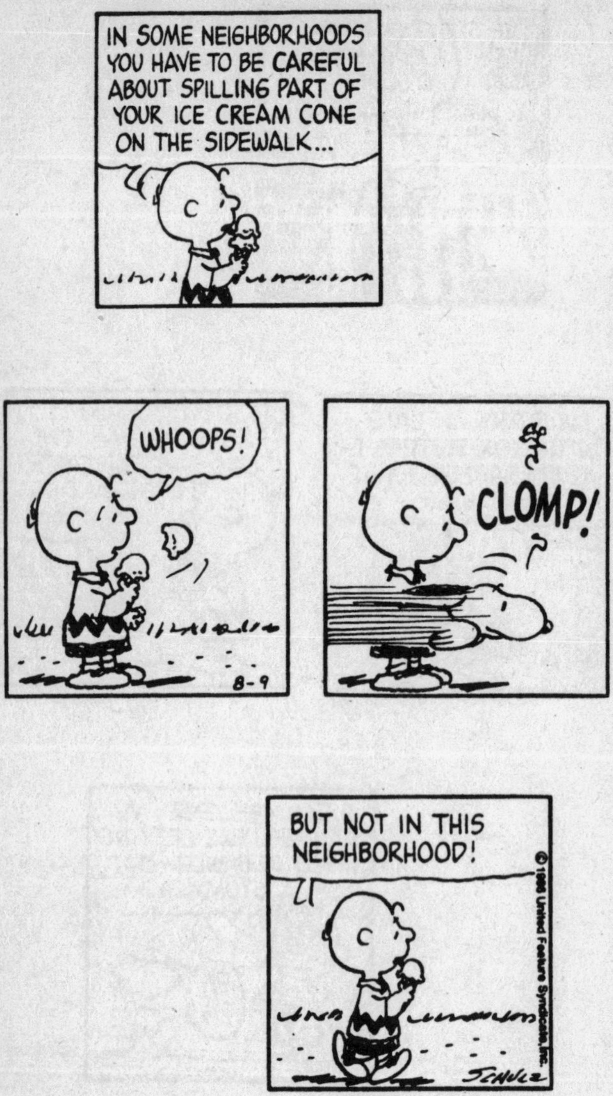
IN SOME NEIGHBORHOODS YOU HAVE TO BE CAREFUL ABOUT SPILLING PART OF YOUR ICE CREAM CONE ON THE SIDEWALK...
WHOOPS!
8-9
CLOMP!
BUT NOT IN THIS NEIGHBORHOOD!
© 1986 United Feature Syndicate, Inc.
SCHULZ

I'VE SPENT HALF MY LIFE STARING AT THAT BACK DOOR WAITING FOR MY SUPPER TO COME OUT..

THAT DOOR IS THIRTY-FIVE INCHES WIDE AND SIXTY-EIGHT INCHES HIGH

IT HAS THREE HINGES.. EACH HINGE HAS FIVE SCREWS ..IT SQUEAKS WHEN IT OPENS AND IT BANGS WHEN IT CLOSES...

8-23

I'M AN EXPERT ON BACKDOORS!

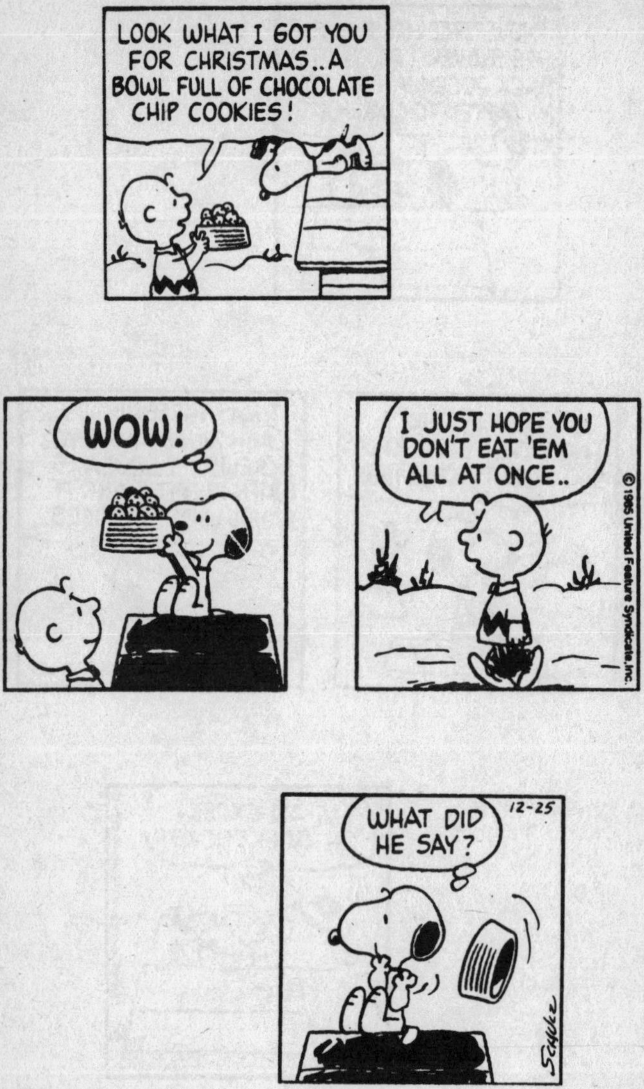
LOOK WHAT I GOT YOU FOR CHRISTMAS..A BOWL FULL OF CHOCOLATE CHIP COOKIES!
WOW!
I JUST HOPE YOU DON'T EAT 'EM ALL AT ONCE..
© 1985 United Feature Syndicate, Inc.
12-25
WHAT DID HE SAY?
SCHULZ

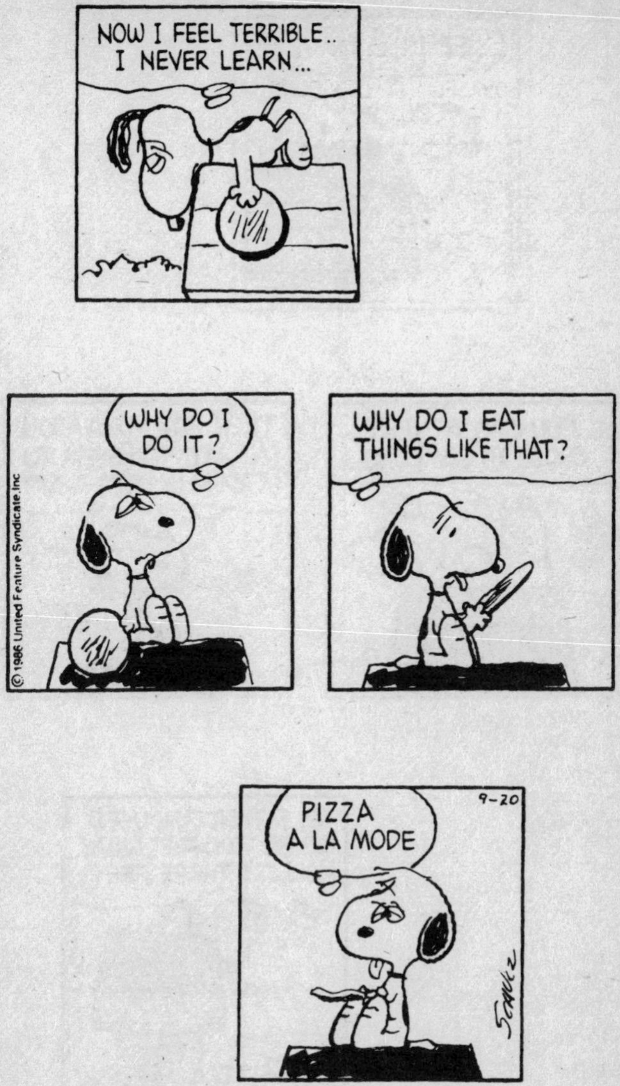
NOW I FEEL TERRIBLE..
I NEVER LEARN...
WHY DO I DO IT?
© 1986 United Feature Syndicate, Inc
WHY DO I EAT THINGS LIKE THAT?
9-20
PIZZA A LA MODE
SCHULZ

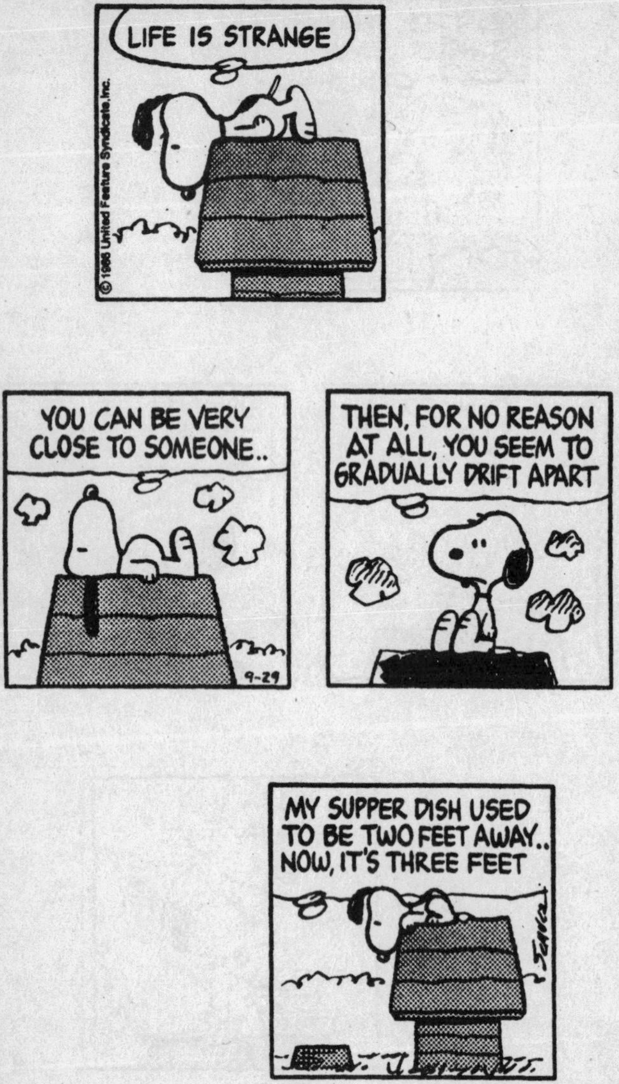
LIFE IS STRANGE
© 1986 United Feature Syndicate, Inc.
YOU CAN BE VERY CLOSE TO SOMEONE..
9-29
THEN, FOR NO REASON AT ALL, YOU SEEM TO GRADUALLY DRIFT APART
MY SUPPER DISH USED TO BE TWO FEET AWAY.. NOW, IT'S THREE FEET

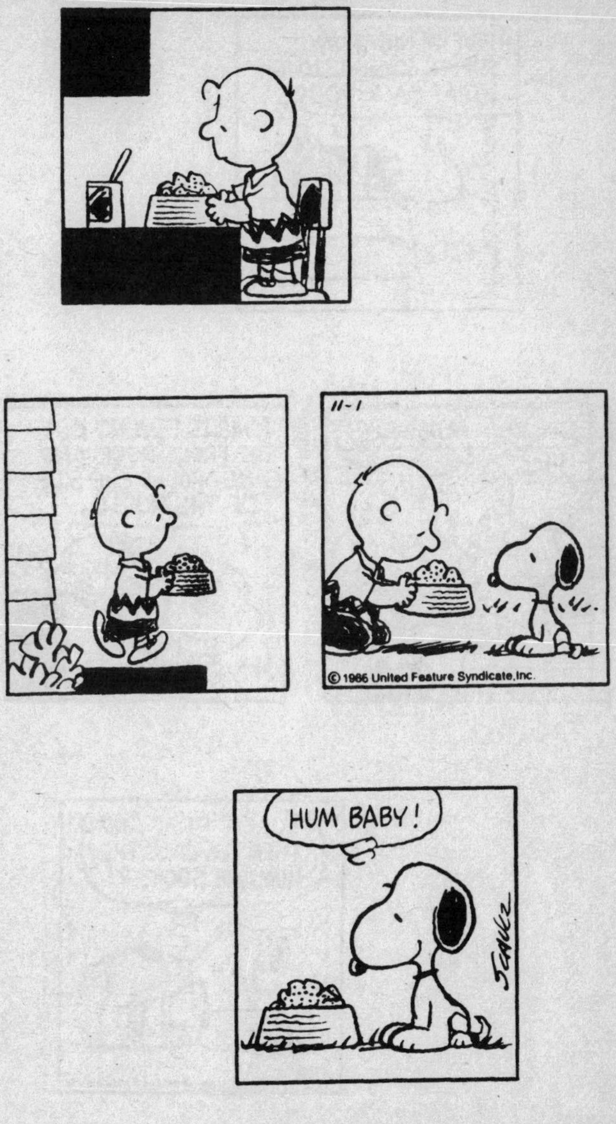
11-1
© 1986 United Feature Syndicate, Inc.
HUM BABY!
SCHULZ

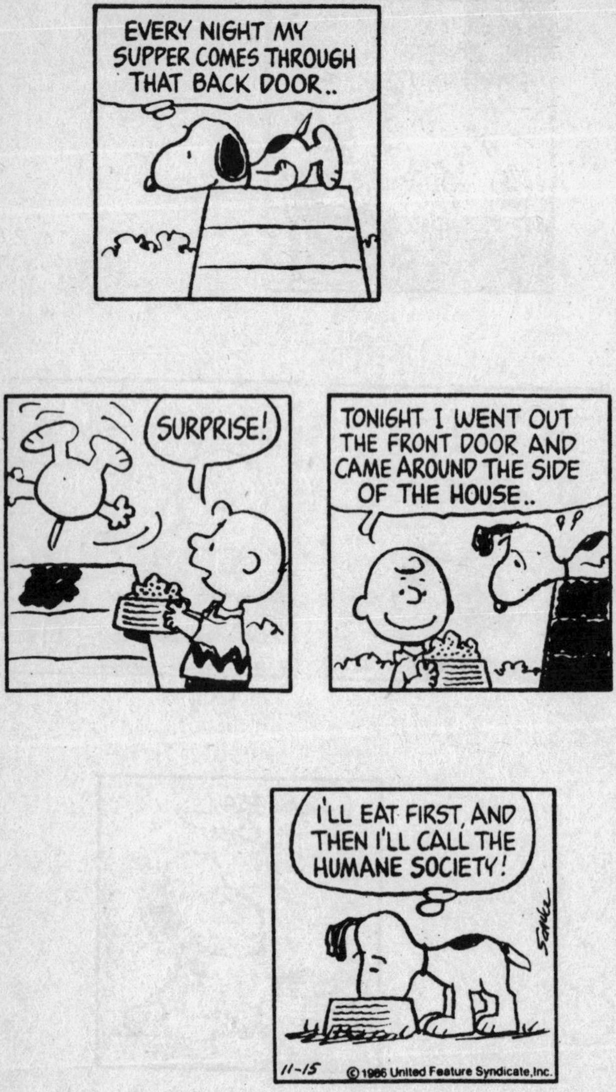
EVERY NIGHT MY SUPPER COMES THROUGH THAT BACK DOOR..
SURPRISE!
TONIGHT I WENT OUT THE FRONT DOOR AND CAME AROUND THE SIDE OF THE HOUSE..
I'LL EAT FIRST, AND THEN I'LL CALL THE HUMANE SOCIETY!
11-15
© 1986 United Feature Syndicate, Inc.

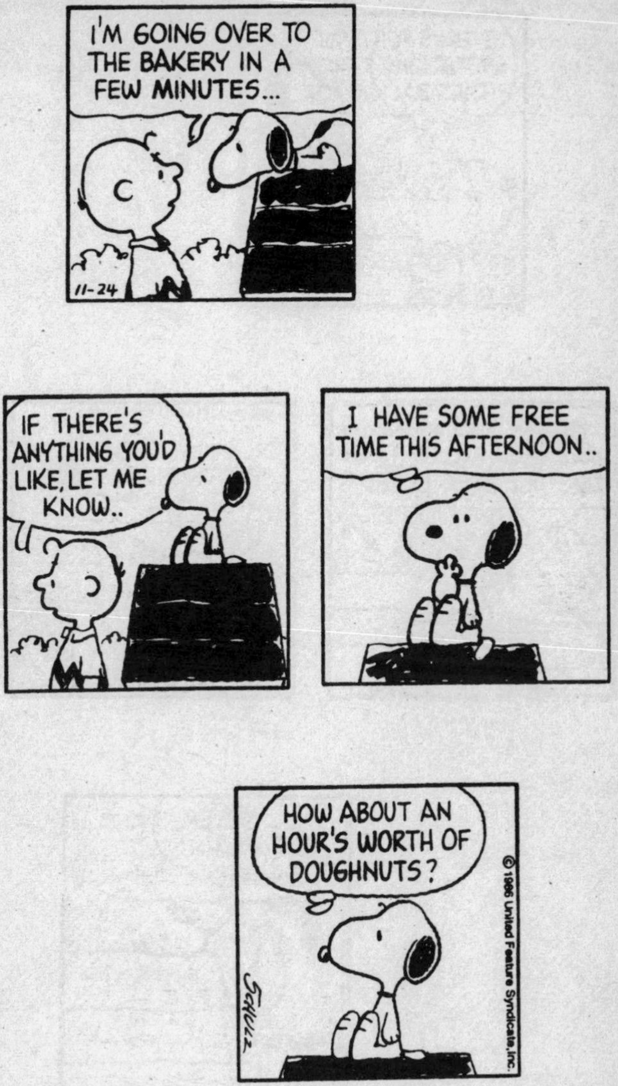
I'M GOING OVER TO THE BAKERY IN A FEW MINUTES...
11-24
IF THERE'S ANYTHING YOU'D LIKE, LET ME KNOW..
I HAVE SOME FREE TIME THIS AFTERNOON..
HOW ABOUT AN HOUR'S WORTH OF DOUGHNUTS?
SCHULZ
© 1986 United Feature Syndicate, Inc.

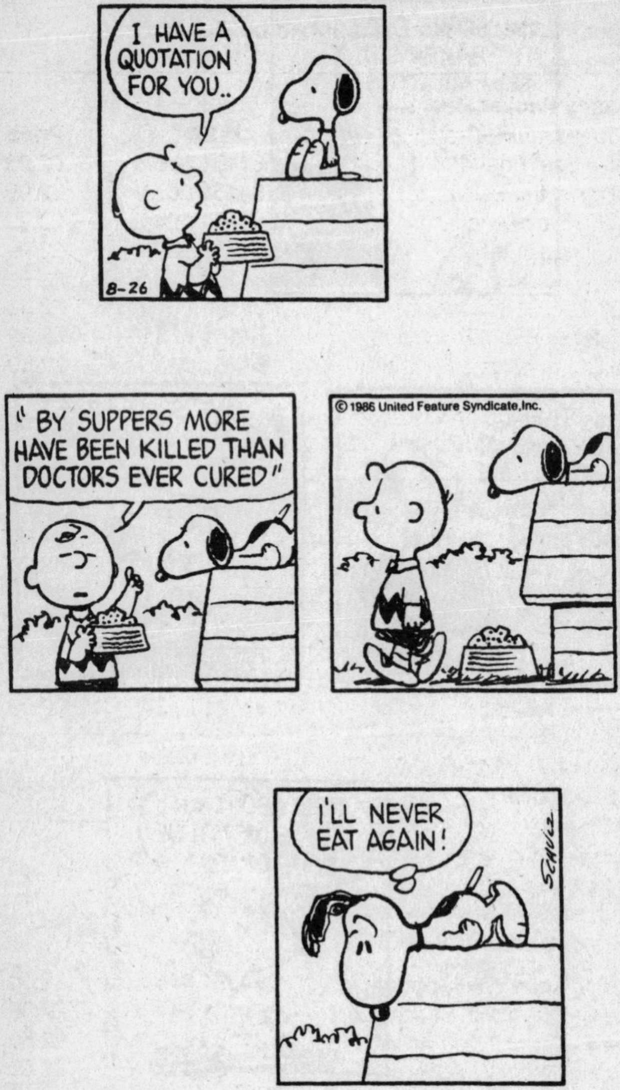
I HAVE A QUOTATION FOR YOU..
8-26
" BY SUPPERS MORE HAVE BEEN KILLED THAN DOCTORS EVER CURED"
© 1986 United Feature Syndicate,Inc.
I'LL NEVER EAT AGAIN!
SCHULZ

Other PEANUTS titles published by Ravette ...

Snoopy Pocket Books
Snoopy features as ...	**ISBN**	**Price**
Man's Best Friend	1 84161 066 6	£2.99
Master of the Fairways	1 84161 067 4	£2.99
The Fearless Leader	1 84161 104 2	£2.99
The Fitness Fanatic	1 84161 029 1	£2.99
The Flying Ace	1 84161 027 5	£2.99
The Great Philosopher	1 84161 064 X	£2.99
The Legal Beagle	1 84161 065 8	£2.99
The Literary Ace	1 84161 026 7	£2.99
The Matchmaker	1 84161 028 3	£2.99
The Music Lover	1 84161 106 9	£2.99
The Sportsman	1 84161 105 0	£2.99

Peanuts 'Little Book' series
Charlie Brown - Wisdom	1 84161 099 2	£2.50
Snoopy - Laughter	1 84161 100 X	£2.50
Lucy - Advice	1 84161 101 8	£2.50
Peppermint Patty - Blunders	1 84161 102 6	£2.50

Peanuts Anniversary Treasury	1 84161 021 6	£9.99
Peanuts Treasury	1 84161 043 7	£9.99

You Really Don't Look 50 Charlie Brown	1 84161 020 8	£7.99

Snoopy's Laughter and Learning series
wipe clean pages
(a fun series of story and activity books for preschool and infant school children)

Book 1 - Read With Snoopy	1 84161 016 X	£2.50
Book 2 - Write With Snoopy	1 84161 017 8	£2.50
Book 3 - Count With Snoopy	1 84161 018 6	£2.50
Book 4 - Colour With Snoopy	1 84161 019 4	£2.50

All PEANUTS™ books are available from your local bookshop or from the address below. Just tick the titles required and send the form with your payment to:-

BBCS, P.O. Box 941, Kingston upon Hull HU1 3YQ
24-hr telephone credit card line 01482 224626

Prices and availability are subject to change without prior notice.

Please enclose a cheque or postal order made payable to BBCS to the value of the cover price of the book and allow the following for postage and packing:-

UK & BFPO:	£1.95 (weight up to 1kg)	3-day delivery
	£2.95 (weight over 1kg up to 20kg)	3-day delivery
	£4.95 (weight up to 20kg)	next day delivery

| EU & Eire: | Surface Mail: | £2.50 for first book & £1.50 for subsequent books |
| | Airmail: | £4.00 for first book & £2.50 for subsequent books |

| USA: | Surface Mail: | £4.50 for first book & £2.50 for subsequent books |
| | Airmail: | £7.50 for first book & £3.50 for subsequent books |

| Rest of the World: | Surface Mail: | £6.00 for first book & £3.50 for subsequent books |
| | Airmail: | £10.00 for first book & £4.50 for subsequent books |

Name: ....

Address: ....

....

....

Cards accepted: Visa, Mastercard, Switch, Delta, American Express

Expiry date .... Signature ....